WINNING THE BANK

CONQUERING CANADA AND THE CLOUD

TRONG NGUYEN

WINNING THE BANK:

CONQUERING CANADA AND THE CLOUD

For information, contact: www.linkedin.com/in/megatrong

Editing by Cabrina Attal, Kathy Clolinger, Carrie Wujek, and Rachel Roberts

Cover Design and Illustrations by Pia Reyes

ISBN: 978-0-9985702-2-8

First Edition: August 2018

This dramatization is inspired by true events. However, certain scenes, characters, names, businesses, incidents, locations and events have been fictionalized for dramatic purposes. The anonymous company that I worked for in this book will, going forward, be known as "Nano."

DEDICATION

This book is dedicated to my parents, Kimba and Duoc, without whom there would be no Trong and no funny stories to tell you.

TABLE OF CONTENTS

FOREWORD

Too often we go through life wishing for things. We wish for material objects, we wish for skills we don't have, and we wish that the situation we are in is different than what it is. The best gift I ever got in life was *nothing*. Having absolutely nothing gave me the drive and determination to chase my dreams and make it a reality. With nothing to lose, I took risks and chances that few others would. With nothing to lose, I had the clarity of thought that I wasn't entitled to anything. If I wanted it, then I would have to work for it.

My story is an extreme one. You don't have to come from abject poverty or flee a war-torn country to realize your dreams. All you need is the conviction to chase your dreams and never give up. In my darkest hours, I never forgot what my biggest heroes told me.

"It's not hard to know where you are going if you know where you came from." – **Duoc & Kimba Nguyen**

CHAPTER 1:

St. John's, Newfoundland

I love money. I love money the way a mother loves her newborn baby. I would sacrifice an arm and your legs to make more money. As far back as I can remember, I've always been obsessed with money. I have no idea why I love money so much, but I do.

Actually, that's bullshit. I know exactly why I dream about money. I grew up dirt poor. I had nothing but the clothes on my back. And even then, those clothes weren't mine. When you grow up in abject poverty, there are only two things you think about – food and money. And I learned to love both! My name is Trong Nguyen, and this is my story.

Trong Nguyen

Have you ever heard of the boat people who came from Vietnam in the late 1970s? I was one of those people. I was only seven or eight at the time, but I remember it like it was yesterday. My parents were typical parents. They wanted to provide a better life for their kids. The war had ravaged the country, destroyed their dreams and left them with nothing but three glimmers of hope – my two sisters and me.

My parents decided that risking everything to escape the oppressive communist regime in Vietnam was worth it if there was a small chance that their kids could have a better life. Like thieves in the night, we snuck out under the cover of darkness. There were no goodbyes, no farewells, and no closure. Closure is therapeutic and emotionally satisfying, but not worth dying for. Fueled by fear and desperation, we crowded onto a small boat with 20 other families and sailed towards a future that was the foundation for all of our nightly prayers.

I don't know how long we were at sea, but it didn't take long for the rickety engine to break down. Put. Put. Put. Kaput. Shit. I didn't know English at the time, but that is what would have come out of my salty mouth if I had. For days and eventually weeks, we were stranded at sea. It seemed like an eternity. Then, finally, hope. Just like Robinson Crusoe, one day we woke up and found ourselves shipwrecked on a pristine and deserted beach. We had made it! We had no idea where we were, but it had to be better than Vietnam.

Somehow, with a sprinkle of the winds and a dusting of luck, we had landed off the coast of Malaysia. We walked along the coastline looking for civilization. To keep us going, we feasted on coconuts for their juice and white meaty goodness. Within days, we hit the jackpot. We ran into people. The Malaysian government was receiving tens of thousands of Vietnamese refugees each month, all with the same misguided nautical plans. They herded and bussed us to refugee camps in Kuala Lumpur.

When we reached the camp, it felt like homecoming. We ran into neighbors, friends and other relatives who must have bought the same shitty boats and maps as we had, because we had all ended up in the same place. We had nothing, but we were the happiest people in the world. The war hadn't killed us. The seas hadn't killed us. At this point, we all decided we were Superman. We were safe, had smiles on our faces, and were completely bulletproof. Make no mistake about it, we were in a make-shift camp. But compared to where we had come from, it felt like a five-star resort.

I was too young to understand it at the time, but the world was opening its hearts and wallets to help people like us. Churches of different denominations around the world were raising money to sponsor families like ours with the intention of giving them a better life. We were sponsored by the Catholic Church in St. John's, Newfoundland. If you don't know where that is, that's ok. No one does. If you look on a map, St. John's is a small city on the easternmost point of Canada. There were only three things you could find in St. John's – snow, cod, and the six new refugees from Vietnam.

Growing up in St. John's was the best thing that ever happened to our family. We were surrounded by white people who spoke a foreign language (literally). Newfies (what we affectionately call the locals) speak in a strange accent with their own lexicon. The accent has two different strands. When they have been drinking a lot, which is often, you can hear twangs of Irish or Scottish descent. That's when it gets really funny because you can't understand a thing they are saying. But what I love about Newfies is that they have the biggest hearts in the world. Through the Church, they raised enough money to put our family up in a house and helped my parents find jobs.

Going to school was a funny experience. For the first while, I couldn't understand a thing anyone was saying. I aced math class because it was just numbers, but for everything else I just sat there as clueless as you could get. Peter Falk would have been proud of my expressions: Columbo had nothing on me. I did what every poor person does when they have no money – I watched TV. I started with the Smurfs, Spiderman and *The Transformers* (the original cartoon from the 1980s). Then I slowly graduated to soap operas with my sisters and aunt. First, it was *Another World*, then *General Hospital*. I was amazed at my transformation. By the time I was ten, I could completely understand English and I started speaking pretty well. But

I was the only ten-year-old I knew who was worried about relationships and what the doctors and nurses in Port Charles were doing. Jell-O Pudding Pops and soaps in the afternoon. Life doesn't get any better than that.

I made friends and started acclimating to the culture. I went to the annual regattas that were so popular in St. John's. I even started going to Cub Scouts and playing floor hockey. My English was improving and I could communicate relatively fluently. My whole family was adapting to the changes as well. There was a small community of Vietnamese refugees and we would get together every weekend to share stories and help each other out. I was so happy and grateful.

At an early age, I found out that I love sales. I love the hustle and I love keeping score. I was 12 years old and we were fundraising for the school. If you sold a certain number of chocolate boxes, you would get a prize. The more boxes you sold, the more and bigger prizes you got. It was that simple. I looked at the list of prizes and my heart started racing. This was awesome! All you had to do was work hard and the school would give you all these amazing prizes. Most of the kids in the class just gave the boxes to their parents to take to work and sell them. Shit. I was already at a disadvantage. My mom was a dishwasher in a restaurant and my dad fixed fridges. Their collars were the wrong color and they didn't work in an office. Undeterred, I went door to door around the neighborhood every night hawking the chocolate boxes. After a few weeks, I was on the leaderboard. I felt vindicated. That's when I first fell in love with sales. I also learned a valuable lesson. No matter what your station in life, if you work hard enough, you can get your reward. No one can stop you.

My parents were Buddhist, but when the Catholic Church sponsored us, they felt indebted to the Church. To show their gratitude, they wanted us to grow up as Catholics. As a result, we went to church every Sunday. I don't remember much about the sermons, but I remember the family that sat in front of us. We always went to the 11 am service and sat in the same spot behind this family. I remember the boy, who was my age, saying to his parents that he couldn't wait for them to go to McDonald's afterwards. And he said it every week. In my little world, I thought these people must be really rich! How do you afford McDonald's every week? Our family only went to McDonald's once every two or three months to celebrate a special occasion. McDonald's was way too expensive. We couldn't afford it. While everyone was busy saying their Our Fathers, I vowed that when I grew up, I was never going to be poor. I was going to have so much money that my kids would be able to go to McDonald's every weekend as well. I was going to be rich.

CHAPTER 2

Pizza And The Colonel

Truth be told, I was a celebrity before I even knew it. When my family and I landed in St. John's, Newfoundland, we were greeted by reporters, media, and everyone who was remotely interested in what kindness looks like when people put their hearts and minds to helping the needy. We had a couple of families that were our primary sponsors. The sponsors helped us with the day-to-day routines and to adjust to life in our new home. If angels existed, we would have called the first one we met Shawn Dobbin.

Shawn was the principal in a high school in St. John's and our primary sponsor. When Shawn opened the door to our new townhouse, we were overcome with emotion. As he led us around I think some of us started to smile, some started to laugh, and my parents started to cry. We were thankful and humbled by our good fortune. We were used to sleeping on dirt floors, fighting for small scraps of nonexistent food and now, overnight, we were living in the lap of luxury. Three small bedrooms, a fridge, and running water. If our friends and relatives in Vietnam could see us now, they would be so jealous!

After a few days, reality set in. We weren't in Vietnam anymore. It was December 1979. It was freezing cold, snow banks were ten Trongs high (I was small back then), and we couldn't understand anything when people spoke to us. Deep down, I think we could have lived with all of that. What we couldn't live with – literally – was the food. When we looked in the fridge, our sponsors had stocked it with everything that they knew to be yummy. There was cheese, French fries, pasta and sausage links. We didn't want to seem ungrateful, but we just didn't know what to do with the food.

My dad met with Shawn and in his broken English, broken French, and with a lot of hand gestures they figured out what the issue was. Before long, we started devouring rice with soy sauce and my mom got the right ingredients for us to cook and eat some traditional Vietnamese food. God bless Shawn.

Slowly but surely, my sisters and I started to get acclimated to our surroundings. We didn't understand the attraction to cheese or drinking milk, but we could see how kids might like chips and French fries. Sadly, our family almost splintered one time because of food. Eight months had passed, and it was my sister's birthday. My parents had worked hard in their blue-collar jobs. Whatever little money they made, they saved every nickel of it. My dad said that we were going to do something special for my sister's birthday. It was going to be the treat of a lifetime.

The entire day, we waited with anticipation. We had a feeling our treat was going to be outrageous. My dad had saved for three months just to have enough money for us to celebrate my sister's birthday in style. At 5pm, my dad left the house and said he was going to get the treat. I played with my sisters and we were giddy with anticipation. We couldn't wait.

Thirty minutes later, we heard the door open and ran as fast as we could. It was party time! My dad was holding a big thin square box. We had no idea what it was. My dad said we were going to love this. He put it on our kitchen table and slowly opened it up like an impresario. We still didn't know what it was. My dad said that a few of his friends at work had introduced him to this. It was called pizza. It was like bread, but they put tomato sauce, some meat and then cheese on top of it. Yuck!

My mom hated it. She couldn't understand why my dad had wasted our hard-earned money on this. My sisters and I weren't sure if we liked it or not, but if mom was boycotting it, then so were we. That was the first time my parents openly fought. I felt bad for my dad. His heart was in the right place. He loved pizza the first time he tried it and thought that we would as well. We laugh at it now, but every food experience we had for the first couple of years was exactly like that.

It wasn't until a few months later that our family came back together as a cohesive unit. It was Christmas time. Other kids were waiting for Santa. The Nguyens? We were waiting for my dad again. He said that he had found something that was completely life-changing. He told us a story about this guy who was in the US military. Apparently, he was very high up in the hierarchy and also an amazing cook. People found out about his hidden talent and he decided to quit the army to open up a chain of restaurants. His name was Colonel Sanders.

The first time we tried Kentucky Fried Chicken was like the first time we ate rice or Pho. Yummy! No matter how bad things got, we knew that everything was going to be alright. We didn't fight that night. We devoured all the chicken, sucked up every piece of fluorescent green coleslaw, and drenched the last piece of fry in as much gravy as we could. When there was nothing left to eat, we all agreed that Canada wasn't such a bad place after all.

CHAPTER 3

Lightning Strikes Twice

It wasn't long before we all started to settle down and find our groove. The Church helped my mom find a job as a dishwasher in a restaurant. My dad did some menial jobs and studied to become a refrigeration technician. At school, I started to make some friends. Everyone in school and in our neighborhood knew who we were and opened their doors and hearts. We were poor, but we were happy and thankful.

Doing homework was an interesting exercise. Every evening, I would sit at the kitchen table and stare blankly at the textbook and notepad. The teachers assigned work to be done for the next day. I was in class and heard everything. Unfortunately, I didn't understand anything. I couldn't ask my parents for help because I never understood what the teacher wanted and hence I couldn't really explain to them what I had to do. My parents told me it was important that I do well in school. It was the only way that I was going to get a good job. They wanted more for me than what they had. My parents never got a university education, so they knew how valuable it was.

I didn't know how I was going to do it, but I wasn't going to let my parents down. I saw how hard they were working just to make ends meet. They weren't going to give up, so neither was I. For the first year, I don't think I ever got any homework done. I would sit at that kitchen table for an hour, staring at the textbook and my notepad. I don't know when it happened, but somewhere along the way, things slowly started to sink in.

My teachers were surprised the first time I started handing in homework. Honestly, so was I. One day it just clicked, and I started understanding what people were saying. Even better than that, I started talking in English and communicating with the other kids. My assignments and grades got better and better. It wasn't long before I was an A student.

I watched TV relentlessly. I studied how people talked, the tone, the intonation, the pitch. If I could help it, I was never going to speak with an accent either. It didn't matter if it was a morning cartoon or an 8 pm drama, I was watching, listening, and studying. I would hear how they talked and then I would repeat it. I didn't know what they were saying, but it didn't matter. It was about sounding like them. I focused on the tone, the inflection, and the pitch.

When you don't know a language or how to communicate with anyone else, you start developing other skills. I started mimicking people. I would watch their mannerisms and body language. I was watching how people talked and what they were saying. I started connecting the dots between words, expressions, and actions. I wouldn't realize until years later that these same skills in reading people are the ones that made me so successful in sales.

I began to read voraciously. I read anything I could get my hands on. If I could help it, I was never going to let vocabulary or language be an inhibitor to my success. I even got the librarian to help me find books that might be interesting for my age group. I was like a mason on a mission. Brick by brick, I was going to build my knowledge and vocabulary. If I didn't know what a word meant, I would just search for it in the dictionary. This was 1983, and there was no such thing as Google. Larry and Sergei were probably at home watching the same shows as I was on TV.

Life was good. Over the next four years we embraced the Canadian culture and our community embraced us. I joined Cub Scouts, played floor hockey and had a bunch of friends to get in trouble with. They taught me how to eat French fries with vinegar and in turn I taught them how to eat Pho. Newfoundland was the best place in the world.

The people were so incredibly nice, and we had everything we could have ever hoped for. I was so grateful that fate had taken us here.

"Kids, come here. Mom and I have something to tell you." With those simple words, I was crushed. To date my world had revolved around the handful of streets that I knew near our house on Chapman Crescent. My dad had just told us that we were moving to Toronto. Apparently, he had given it a lot of thought and there were more and better jobs in Toronto. Even though we were only in elementary school, he was thinking about our future and wanted my sisters and me to go to the best universities in Canada. Many of the best universities in Canada were in Ontario. To my dad, it was a no-brainer – it would be dumb if we didn't move to Toronto for the opportunities. My sisters and I were in complete shock. In a period of five years, our world would turn upside down not once, but twice. And they say lightning never strikes the same place twice.

CHAPTER 4

Back To Sea

My dad bought a van, we sold the few possessions that we had, and we packed the remainder in every nook and cranny we could find in the van. With lots of hugs and sad goodbyes, we started making the long road trip to Toronto. Our sponsors were like reluctant empty-nesters sending their kids off to university. They cried and wished us the best. This time around we got closure with all of our friends and neighbors. We didn't sneak off in the middle of the night but started our journey with the sun at our backs as we headed west to our new home. I remember being sad and angry. I didn't want to leave St. John's. It was the best place to grow up as a kid. I put up a good front, smiling a lot and saying I was looking forward to the journey. But behind closed doors or when I was by myself, when no one was looking, I cried.

We were back at sea. Instead of salt water, we were drowning in cars on a sixteen-lane highway called the 401. Highway 401 is the main road that cuts Toronto in half. To get from the east end to the west end, it was your only practical option. Dorothy, we aren't in Kansas anymore. As a kid, it's really hard to describe the overwhelming feeling you get when you come from a small town in Newfoundland to arriving in Toronto. No one was saying anything in the van, but I knew that we were all doing the same thing – panicking.

My dad, through his connections and friends, was able to rent an apartment for us in the Caledonia area of Toronto. My dad's friends assured us that we had an amazing apartment. They lived in the same building and could vouch for it. I don't know what we were expecting, but we were stunned when we finally got there. I think all of us were envisioning an urban version of the "niceness" that we had in Newfoundland. Instead, we got a stinky, dirty, dingy three-bedroom condo infested with ants and cockroaches. Our mouths dropped open and our facial expressions gave it all away. We were completely horrified.

At that time, the Caledonia neighborhood (between Lawrence and Dufferin) was a sketchy area populated with low-income housing and the characters to match it. I don't know why I was surprised we were living there, because we didn't have a lot of money anyway. That was what we could afford. Everyone else in the building was exactly like us. They were poor immigrants and refugees who had moved to Toronto in hope of a better opportunity. It was the Canadian version of Harlem, the Bronx, or Hell's Kitchen when those places were sketchy. At one point, I had more cockroaches living with me in my bedroom than I had friends.

My family and I hunkered down and did what we did best: we survived. We cleaned up the apartment as best as we could. My mom got a job in a plastics factory and my dad got a job as a refrigeration technician. My sisters and I made new friends and put all our energies into school. The neighborhood wasn't very safe, so we beelined it home every day and stayed locked in our apartment. We kept our noses to the grindstone and didn't complain. We knew our parents were doing the best that they could with what they had. They were trying to make ends meet and we were going to do our part to meet them half-way. Complaining wasn't going to make the situation any better. The only thing that could do that was money – and we didn't have any. Or did we?

Six months later.

"Kids, we are moving!" my dad proclaimed one night at dinner. Yes! Hallelujah! We all started crying. This time around, it was tears of joy. We couldn't believe our good fortune. I don't know how my dad did it, but he had scrimped and saved every penny that he had made over the last five years. Unbeknownst to us, those pennies had snowballed into a down payment that we could make towards a new house. Like the Jeffersons in that classic TV show, we were "moving on up."

My dad had scoped out a posh suburb called Scarborough. I say posh, because everything is relative. When you come from the ghetto of Toronto, then it's fair to call Scarborough posh. I didn't realize it at the time, but Scarborough was one of those suburbs that people make fun of. If you said you were from Scarborough, everyone knew that you were poor and lower income. It was a fair assessment because it was true. I didn't care, though. Scarborough was ten times better than where we had just come from.

CHAPTER 5

Brebeuf College

My sisters and I took to Scarborough like fish to water. We quickly made new friends and adjusted to our new school and surroundings. In a blink, I breezed through grades seven and eight. Choosing a high school was a big decision that would change the trajectory of my life forever. At the time, there were a handful of good high schools near our house. I chose to go to an all-boys Catholic high school called Brebeuf College. It was founded by Jesuit priests and was known as a breeding ground for future leaders. Brebeuf only accepted students with strong academic backgrounds and a desire to make a difference.

Everyone dressed in a school uniform and there were three mandatory pillars to life at Brebeuf. First was the academics. The school only focused on core subjects such as math, science, and the languages. If you wanted to attend a class in shop or home economics, you would have to go elsewhere. Second was the athletics. You were "highly" encouraged to get involved and participate in a sport. The faculty and administration rightfully believed that physical activity was good for the body as well as the mind. Third was service. You were required to give back to the community and do volunteer work.

At Brebeuf, you couldn't help but notice that there were a lot of affluent students. They were the rich kids straight out of the movies *Sixteen Candles* or *Pretty in Pink*. They drove to school in a BMW or Mercedes that their parents gave them. If you were middle class, then you drove a domestic car made from one of the Detroit automakers. I took the TTC (public transit) an hour each way every day just to get to school. These kids had a weekly allowance equivalent to a king's ransom, while I worked in a grocery store making minimum wage stocking produce. I wasn't angry or jealous. Alright, I was jealous, but I was also even more motivated. I decided to double down on hard work and school.

Academically, I decided to focus my energies on math and liberal arts. I figured this would be the best foundation for going into business. I had heard that if you wanted to do well in business, you had to have excellent communication skills. This meant I had to have perfect English, both speaking and writing skills. Luckily for me, Brebeuf had one of the best English departments in Toronto.

Brebeuf also offered something that only a few privileged schools in Toronto offered – Latin. Latin was a mandatory language class in grade nine and optional after that. Latin is the foundation for all of the romance languages. If you wanted to master English, taking Latin would provide you with a foundation and path to get there. My friends laughed at me, but I decided to take Latin right throughout high school. They couldn't understand why I was studying a language no one used anymore. I never told them, but I was studying Latin so that I could get better in English. In Latin class, we conjugated words and translated the classics until we were blue in the face. Two or three times a week I would go to Mrs. Coughlin for extra help so that I could ace the class. Latin was dead to everyone else, but it was my lifeline to mastering English.

When I wasn't working at my part-time job or running track or cross-country at school, I studied. I studied my butt off. I spent every waking hour making sure that I aced all of my classes and got the highest marks that I could. You couldn't get into the best universities unless you had the highest marks. I wasn't leaving anything to chance. My parents had worked too hard to get me here, so I wasn't going to squander this opportunity.

Graduation was a bittersweet moment. Four years flew by faster than a speeding bullet. I met some amazing new friends and was sad that I would be leaving most of them. Once we parted ways, who knew if we would ever see each other again. Brebeuf lived up to its reputation of being one of the best high schools in Toronto. I learned the importance of giving back, I saw what sports can do to foster teamwork and comradery, but more importantly, I saw what you can achieve with hard work and perseverance.

As it was a Catholic school, it was appropriate that we had our graduation ceremony in a church. I got dressed in the only suit that I had. My family sat next to me. It was a proud moment for all of us. Our valedictorian gave a rousing speech about what we had just accomplished and what was in store for our future. Our department heads got up and gave the academic honors for the highest marks in their respective subjects. We were all anxious and excited for what lay ahead. I had gotten straight As. I had scrapped, clawed, and worked my butt off and it had all paid off.

"And the academic award for the highest mark in Latin goes to Trong Nguyen."

I couldn't believe it. I ran up to the podium and gave Mrs. Coughlin a big hug as she handed me the award. I went home that night and couldn't stop smiling. I was so thankful for where I was right now. I had just graduated from one of the best high schools in Toronto. A week earlier, I had gotten an acceptance letter from the University of Western Ontario with an academic scholarship. Everything that my parents had sacrificed so much for was about to become a reality. I was ready. Now it was my turn to carry the torch.

CHAPTER 6

Homecoming

Twenty years later.

Air Canada Flight 706 landed and slowly taxied to the gate at Toronto Pearson International Airport. It was 25 degrees Celsius outside and the sun was shining. Damn. I was so used to the Fahrenheit system, I was going to have to do that mental conversion in my head until I knew automatically what 25 degrees felt like.

Most people would have been ecstatic and elated. For the first time in a long time, I was going to be in the same city as my parents, and they were going to see their grandchildren more than once a year. I was coming home. I don't know what I was feeling, but it wasn't excitement or joy. As I rode the escalators down to Immigration, it finally hit me like a punch from Mike Tyson when he ruled the world. I didn't feel Canadian anymore.

For the last 16 years, I had been living in a posh suburb of Chicago. I had dined in the finest restaurants, driven around in my Porsche 911, and made more money than Warren Buffet. Alright, I'm messing with you. For the last decade, I had been busy being an absentee husband so that my wife could raise our three kids as a single parent while I traveled all over the US for my job. We had been driving around in a minivan, and the closest we ever got to fine dining was takeout at Little Caesar's down the street. Raising three young kids is incredibly hard work. Dammit, someone was always in diapers. But I digress.

There are three main reasons why I love the US so much. The first is that it offers so many opportunities. If you have a dream and are willing to work for it, you can get yours or do whatever you want to do. The second reason is the American spirit. There is definitely something ingrained in the American psyche about getting up after you have been knocked down. Everyone loves a comeback story. Americans see failure as a rite of passage or just a stepping stone to success. I love that! The third reason – and probably the most important reason – is because of Amazon. I love the fact that you can buy anything you ever want online and have it at your doorstep within five minutes. Instant gratification: it's the American way.

As I was riding in the taxi from the Toronto airport, I was blown away by all the new buildings. It looked like the city was engulfed with new condos everywhere. My driver told me that a small two-bedroom condo would cost about $1M. Damn. Almost New York prices. As I saw our reflections streaming by in the glass buildings, I started to reflect on how I got here. I left Chicago on a high note. I had just closed a deal with one of the largest health insurance companies and moved them to the cloud. I had helped rewrite the book on regulatory and compliance at Nano Software and had paved the way for other healthcare companies to move to the cloud. From a professional perspective, for the third time in my life, I was about to drop everything and start completely anew. When I left Canada 20 years ago, I said that hell would have to freeze over before I would come back. Shoot. It's starting to feel really cold now.

I met my boss Andrea Montroy, about eight years ago. We hit it off right away. I wouldn't admit it to my wife at the time, but I looked up to Andrea. She was my hero. We were like Mick Jagger and Keith Richards of The Rolling Stones. I was the smart front man and Andrea was the one with grit and talent. We loved fast cars, fast money, and closing deals. That was the glue that held us together. I idolized Andrea. She had all the toys that I wanted to have and ran a business with skills that I knew I would never have. What made Andrea truly special was that she deeply cared about people and was authentic.

Watching Andrea work is like watching Michelangelo paint. One time we were in our account planning sessions, where each sales rep stands up for 45–60 minutes in front of the whole team to talk about their customers and how much revenue they are planning to extract from each one. The sales rep walks through their detailed plans for said monetary extraction. The rest of the team then gets a chance to question the strategy and approach so that everyone is aligned and knows their roles. One of the sales reps stood up and started going through his presentation. We were all listening intently. Andrea then interjected and started pulling on a piece of thread about a certain revenue number for this specific customer. Within five minutes, she had completely unraveled the account plan. But she did it with a smile and wasn't mean about it. She did it in a way that you could learn from, and you wanted to come back and do it better the next time because you didn't want to let her down. That was the magic of Andrea.

Andrea was a rising star, and everyone loved her. They loved her craziness and authenticity. She was an oxymoron and contradiction in so many ways, and yet it all somehow seemed to work. Andrea got promoted and the leadership team at Nano was grooming her for the next level of leadership. They asked her to move to Canada and right a sinking ship. Like all good sales people, she didn't flinch. For the right price, Andrea would do anything! She packed her bags and caught the next flight to Toronto.

Nano Canada had a storied and checkered past. It was a Canadian subsidiary headquartered in Toronto and over the last five years had seen its fair share of turmoil. There had been various shenanigans at the leadership level. One played games with customer contracts. Another slept with a few people he really shouldn't have. And most of the middle management team was gaming the system so they could get their big fat bonuses to the detriment of the company. There were groups, cliques and fiefdoms. And if you didn't belong to the right group, you were screwed. There was definitely no upward mobility in your future. Everyone in the subsidiary felt it was completely OK to misbehave. It got so bad that a lot of them thought it was just standard operating procedure.

Boy, were they in for a rude awakening! Andrea was being brought in to clean house and turn the ship around. And as her trusted lieutenant, I was part of the new vanguard. I was going to mop, vacuum, paint, and do whatever it took to help Andrea clean house.

CHAPTER 7

The New Team

Canadians love Americans the way most Asians love the Chinese. They don't. To be fair, both relationships are a bit more nuanced than just love or hate. Canadians have always been the little brother to the US. Canadians have a well-earned reputation for being nice, thoughtful and open to embracing diverse ethnic groups and cultures. They look after every citizen with universal healthcare and educate everyone who wants to be educated – regardless of socioeconomic level. No one is left behind.

Yet in today's world, that doesn't really mean squat. It's about consumption and how big your economy is. And the US is the king of consumption and making everything bigger. The relationship has always been marked by a mix of awe and respect, sprinkled with a minor dose of jealousy. Canadians view the Americans the way I view the Chinese. I like everything about the Chinese. I am amazed by their contributions to society. But deep down, I would be disingenuous if I didn't admit that I was a little bit jealous. I'm jealous of what they have and what they have accomplished.

I started my career working at Canadian subsidiaries of US-based companies. That usually means that the Canadian subsidiary plays second fiddle to the US. This has always grated on most of the people I have worked with in Canada. Due to currency fluctuations and the size of the Canadian economy, our deals were always smaller. And if your deals are smaller, you get fewer resources, less respect and even lesser pay. We always hated when Americans came up, did their fly-by, prescribed how we should fix our business, and then went home. Damn Americans. And now I was one of them.

My predecessor was highly regarded within Nano. He had been around for a while. His departure was abrupt and unexpected. There were rumors that it was because of an excessive expense violation with a stripper named Candi. I had to smile, as I can imagine the mischief that must have gone on. Any sales rep worth their weight has a thousand ways to hide a few hundred or thousand dollars in their expense account, so this must have been in the tens of thousands of dollars. Totally egregious, but definitely funny. On the bright side, I'm sure Candi was able to pay for her first-year tuition in nursing school. Meanwhile, I had inherited his team and was about to get a handle on what I would be working with.

All our introductory meetings and knowledge transfer sessions were scheduled over a couple of weeks. We had some group meetings and numerous 1:1s. The team was judging me as much as I was judging them. Over the weeks, I nodded my head a lot but didn't say much. I think some of them thought I was even-tempered and measured. They were so wrong. In general, I don't say that much anyway. But don't mistake introversion for being mild-tempered and on an even keel. Anyone who knows me would never accuse me of that. A sideway glance here, crossed arms there – I could tell that they were still suspicious of me: another American coming up, doing his tour of duty for 2–3 years, and then bolting out of here again. I'd been in their shoes. I knew what they were thinking.

Overall, I was impressed with the team. In general, they had decent skills, were good-natured, and had a strong desire to make a difference. Rudderless for a long time, they just didn't know how to win. Over the years, they seemed to develop decent relationships with the customer at the lower- and middle-management levels but hadn't found a way to break through to the executive and C-Suite. To a certain extent, they also seemed afraid to rock the boat and shake the status quo. That was perfectly fine with me, as I majored in glass breaking in grad school.

All large enterprise software companies operate the same way. Nano is no different. Each sales rep looking after a large global client runs a big team that includes sales, services, operations, and marketing. That's their core team and their de facto family. But they also belong to another team. This team consists of peers who look after other large customers. You don't really interact with this team of peers all that much. If anything, you compete with them on a daily basis for resources, funding, etc. In that regard, it is almost a zero-sum game. This team of peers is then led by a director of sales. The banking team in Nano Canada is considered the most seasoned team in the company. They had to be exceptional at what they did, because banking customers were the toughest in the world and they also brought in the most revenue. We were the best and brightest that Nano Canada had to offer.

Abe Scheinberg was our boss. The first time we all met Abe at The Irish Embassy in downtown Toronto, we did a double take. We were all dressed in suits and ready to impress our new boss. If you were in the financial district and you looked after banks for a living, how else would you dress? Abe showed up at the restaurant in jeans, a T-shirt and sandals. If we had known him a bit better, we would have laughed ourselves silly and ridden his butt all night. Instead, we kept a straight face and kissed the ring. Abe was in his early thirties, dressed like he was in his twenties and, without his beard, looked like he was in his teens. One thing we all agreed on was that Abe was wicked smart. He had a brain that Spock would envy.

It was a ragtag team. We were more like the dirty half dozen. We were all so different – in both our styles and our approaches to sales. But what was indisputable was that we were all highly effective and successful in our own ways. We were like Karl "The Mailman" Malone from the Utah Jazz – we always delivered.

CHAPTER 8

OSFI

To an outsider, computers and high tech can seem ridiculously complicated. Geeky engineers develop, build, and then market the products. Until Steve Jobs came along, computers were more mysterious than black magic. I will tell you a dark secret about the high-tech industry: we purposely make it complicated for our customers. If it was simple, they wouldn't need to spend millions of dollars on our solutions. And if they didn't spend millions of dollars buying our products, the high-tech companies wouldn't need us sales reps. I'm being defensive and rationalizing in a self-preserving way, but I might just think that is a bad thing.

In general, this is how it works. Companies such as Nano make either hardware or software. Customers may or may not need professional services and help to install and make these components work together. When you combine the hardware, software and services together, you get a complete solution.

In the past, customers would install these solutions in their data centers and run them. In the 1990s, companies such as IBM and others realized that they could make a lot more money by hosting and running these solutions for their customers in their private data centers. They called it outsourcing and marketed the heck out of it. The tagline was: "We can run it cheaper, faster, and better than you can ever do it on your own. We do this for a living. Leave it to the professionals." Poof! All of a sudden, IBM, CSC, EDS and a slew of wannabes added billions of incremental revenues to their books. It was magic.

In the early 2000s, software companies and their growth rates started to slow down. They had feasted on customers' fears of the year 2000 (Y2K) but now the party was over. The year 2000 came and went and nothing happened. Nothing broke and the world didn't end. With increased expectations from Wall Street, high-tech companies scrambled to find their next billion dollars in revenue to justify their sky-high earnings multiples. That's when companies such as Nano, Amazon, and Oracle came up with a brilliant plan to help their customers reach the next level of efficiency. They called it the CLOUD. It was hot and sexy. The tagline was: "We can run it cheaper, faster, and better than your outsourcer. We do this for a living. Leave it to the *real* professionals." Poof! All of a sudden, IBM, CSC, EDS and the other companies that had been feeding at the trough of outsourcing for the last decade were scrambling and saying, "What the hell?"

When I joined Nano, it was just starting its journey to the cloud. It was apparent early on that this would be the next wave of technology. The excitement was intoxicating. I was drinking the Kool-Aid as I hawked it to my customers. I was going to convert every last customer to the cloud. And then reality hit. Marketing the cloud was one thing. Selling it and closing deals were totally different. Little did I realize that it's actually quite complicated. Most large companies have numerous regulatory and compliance laws that they have to meet. Healthcare and the finance industries are probably the most highly regulated. They have to prove to government and regulatory bodies that they know where their data is at all times, who has access to it, and provide recovery plans in case something disastrous happens. And they have to prove all of this with extensive audit reports. So, if we were going to sell to these customers, we would have to prove that we could do all this for them and more. Then, and only then would they move to the cloud. Shit. Double shit.

It took me two years, but I was able to convince the largest healthcare company in the US to move to the cloud. I had learned a lot and had all the scars to prove it. The work I did became the foundation for Nano's legal compliance language for all their contracts with healthcare customers. Fresh off this win, I had all the confidence and background to go change the banking industry.

Nate Larramore is the senior counsel at Nano Canada. Born and raised in Toronto, he went to Queen's University in Kingston, Ontario and graduated top of his class in law school. After a decade at one of the most prestigious law firms, Nate decided to join the corporate world and make time for family instead. I knew that if I was going to win a banking customer, Nate and I would have to be two peas in a pod. We would have to be simpatico in our approach and strategy. It was the same strategy I had run with the healthcare company in the US and it had turned out to be highly successful. I made an appointment to see Nate and talk about how we could go attack the banks together.

After a few minutes of pleasantries, I walked Nate through the different strategies that I used to win over the healthcare regulators in the US and how those strategies could be applied to banking regulators in Canada and the US. The Office of the Superintendent of Financial Institutions (OSFI) in Canada is the main regulatory body providing guidance for anything and everything banks are allowed to do in Canada. If we couldn't crack OSFI, we were never going to win and move the banks to the cloud. I had done it before with tough as nails regulators in the US and I knew we could do it here. After listening to me for ten minutes, Nate looked at me stony-eyed and turned on me like a caged animal.

"I'm sick and tired of you Americans coming up here and telling us what to do. You guys have no idea what you are doing. The Canadian marketplace is different and what worked for you in the States is not going to work here. Why don't you do your couple years, get your ticky mark, and go back to the States?"

I could feel my blood pressure rising. What did the doctor say to do? Breathe. Breathe. One. Two. Three. Four. Five. Six. Seven. Eight. Nine. Ten.

"Nate, I don't know who you think you are talking to, but I'm Canadian."

With that, I stood up and walked out of his office. Asshole.

CHAPTER 9

Take It To The Max

In large high-tech companies, there comes a point when the product lines get so complicated and varied that they set up a customer support structure with an overarching client relationship owner (client director) and different business units (sales specialists) who work hand in hand to support the customers' needs. Like most sports, you can't have the best teams unless you have the best individual contributors. The best players, with the right coaching and direction, guarantee you a win nine times out of ten. In every major deal I've done at Nano, I've always had a great support team: teammates I can depend on to get things done without having it all blow up on us.

Max Richard was my cloud specialist. I was skeptical the first time I met him. I wasn't sure I liked him, but I was definitely jealous. The guy had everything going on. I wanted to get to know him better, so I arranged a lunch meeting. Ki was one of my new favorite sushi restaurants near our downtown office. I got there ten minutes early (like I always do) and got a table near the window. I ordered my usual – Tanqueray and tonic with a lime. As I was waiting, I heard this loud squeal from a nearby motorcycle. Some idiot on a Ducati 996 was speeding and came to an abrupt stop right in front of the restaurant. What a douche.

I went back to my phone and started going through emails.

"Hi Trong. I'm Max."

Shit. Just my luck. I looked up and it was the douchebag. He was dressed in an impeccable Italian suit and carrying his motorcycle helmet. I extended my hand as a gesture of goodwill.

"Hi Max. I'm Trong."

When he started speaking, in my mind I rolled my eyes even more. He had this great French accent. No matter what he said, it just sounded good. And to top it all off, he had this great head of hair. Curly black locks of hair. It was the type of hair that girls fawn over and guys wish they had.

I was so jealous. I was beginning to hate his guts. God, please tell me he's not smart. That would just be cruel.

Over lunch, I learned that Max was the embodiment of his name. He was an adrenaline junkie and loved to live life to the fullest. He grew up in Montreal and had been with Nano for 15 years. He loved heli-skiing, rode his motorcycle faster than he should and was thinking of taking up long-distance bicycle riding to get more exercise. Max had two kids, his wife was a doctor and they lived in downtown Toronto. Max was an engineer by training and within five minutes of talking to him, I knew he was really smart.

I walked Max through my plan of methodically and strategically going after the bank and moving them to the cloud. I told him that I needed his help and that I couldn't do it alone. This was going to be a Herculean effort, and everyone was going to have to be fully committed for us to win. Max was enthusiastic and said that he was excited by the opportunity. I liked what I heard. I could tell that Max had been around the block a few times. I love working with smart people because it makes life that much easier. We shook hands and left the restaurant ready to climb Mount Everest together.

The Bank of Upper Canada (or, as they call it in Canada, BUC) was founded in 1860 and since its inception it has been a pillar of strength and financial prowess in Canada. Headquartered in Toronto, it has over 90,000 employees around the world. Over the last decade, with a revered and beloved CEO, it had gone on a massive mergers and acquisitions binge. In a short period of time, BUC became a powerhouse in North America. It gobbled up small regional banks in the US when those banks were teetering on the brink. BUC was very conservative in nature and its CEO prided himself on not investing or going into any business that he couldn't understand. So, when the subprime mess hit the US, BUC came out of it relatively unscathed with its balance sheet that much stronger to pursue even more acquisitions.

BUC was my only customer, so I either sank or swam with it. I started doing research and absorbing as much material and background as I could find. I talked to partners. I talked to my internal teams to get their thoughts and perspectives. I started to talk to BUC contacts at the lowest levels. I wanted to make sure I had as much data as possible to do my analysis. I was using every skill and framework I learned in business school to make sense of BUC and how Nano could further their business. For a period of a month, every breakfast, lunch and dinner were with customers. I was immersing myself into their company and culture and loving every minute of it. With everyone I met, I talked about the same thing – the CLOUD. I talked about what it was and how it could transform the bank. Before long, I noticed that there was a small buzz starting to emanate from the bank about the cloud. I was starting to hear some of the things I was telling them bouncing back at me verbatim. It was starting to work.

One thing that I noticed was plainly absent was Max. He was supposed to be my right-hand man, but I don't think he had one conversation about the cloud with the bank. We were going to fix that. I called him for a one-on-one meeting.

"Max, I don't understand. When we talked, we both agreed that we were going to go attack and win BUC. I've been working my ass off meeting as many customers as possible. I don't think you met one customer at BUC over the last month. Am I missing something?"

I already knew the answer. I was pleading with him for help more than anything else. I knew that I couldn't do this alone. I had already done it once with a healthcare customer and that was enough pain and misery to last a lifetime. It took nearly all of my blood, sweat and tears to do it.

"Trong, I'm so sorry, man. The last month has been crazy. We just finished our year end and I had a bunch of loose ends to tie up. I'm on it. We'll go take this bank down," Max replied.

OK. I totally understood that. These things happen. Priorities happen. I let the situation go but was going to monitor it. Three weeks later. Nada. Crickets. Max hadn't made one call to BUC. Now I was pissed. I called another one-on-one meeting with Max. Before my meeting, I started to do a bit of digging to see what the disconnect was. What I discovered was that over the last 18 months, Max and the team had already launched an all-out assault on BUC to move them to the cloud. There was a bunch of promising conversations, there was some executive support, and then everything fizzled and died on the vine. Max was emotionally spent and wasn't ready to get back on the horse and ride it again.

"Max, I'm going to be transparent with you. I know what you've been through the last 18 months. I need your help. When I say I am all in, I'm all in. I will bleed to make a deal happen. I know how to win and how we can get BUC to the cloud. I've done it before. I need you to be all in. I can't do this alone. I don't want you to answer me now. I want you to think about it. And when you are ready and have made your decision, come back and we'll talk. If you can't be all in, I'll understand. I'll talk to our VP and have another resource assigned to the team."

A week later, Max invited me to lunch. After the initial pleasantries, Max told me that he was all in. He told me about the last 18 months and how he was hesitant to get back in the saddle. He had done his own research on me and talked to some of his peers in the US. They had confirmed what I had told him. I would bleed to make a deal happen. He was going to be all in. I was relieved to hear those words come out of his mouth. I knew that, without him, we would never be able to get a deal done.

Little did I realize that Max and I would later become best friends. Over the next year, we would spend more time with each other than with our wives and families. Somehow, somewhere, someway, we would crack the code and win the bank.

CHAPTER 10

Putting The Pieces Together

Day by day, week by week, I was slowly building up my list of contacts and correlating my data. I was starting to get a picture of how the people ran the bank and the politics that ran the people. I was ebbing and flowing in a way that would make Frank and Claire Underwood proud. People have always been amazed at the way I can navigate customer politics with the same hustle as an up-and-coming congressman fighting for his seat in a tight election. I always smile and take the compliment with a dose of humility.

The truth is, it's easy. If you are good at reading people (and all good sales reps are), all you have to do is talk to a lot of people and triangulate the data. Figure out who is lying and who is telling you the truth. And with a big enough sample size, you'll have enough data to put all the pieces of the mosaic together. Like the rest of sales, it's just a numbers game.

Sean O'Reilly was our designated executive sponsor at BUC. He had played this role for the last five years and relished his position of influence and responsibility. I liked Sean a lot. On the surface, Sean and I seemed to be from two different worlds. I weighed 130 lbs. soaking wet, looked completely GQ in my custom-made suits and naturally gravitated towards sparkling wine. Sean easily weighed 230 lbs., bought his suits at Tip Top, and drank copious amounts of anything. I was quiet and reserved, while Sean was always the life of the party. He always had an opinion and wasn't shy to share it with you or blog about it.

The one thing that Sean and I both shared was that we came from humble beginnings and never forgot it. It was the crucible moment that defined our character and outlook on life. Sean gave me the lay of the land at the bank: who did what and who were the real power players that an org chart wouldn't reveal. After a month, when Sean felt I was ready, he introduced me to his boss, Nick Bauer.

Nick was a long-time executive at another bank and had come over to BUC five years ago to help the bank transform into a customer service juggernaut.

I could tell Nick didn't like me the moment he laid eyes on me. At our meeting, Nick was direct in telling me that nothing gets done without his support and approval. Everything stops with him. Nick went on to inform me that Nano software sucked and that he had different plans for the bank. Nick was going to take the bank down a path with Cisco, Avaya and others. Working with Nick was going to be very interesting.

Nick reported to another SVP named John Thompson. John was definitely an acquired taste. He must have made a lot of money in his past ventures. Weekends and free time were spent on his 60-foot yacht. John was the first executive to be recruited by BUC and then promptly brought over Nick and Sean. Both were trusted and loyal lieutenants.

I was sitting across from John. His disdain for sales reps was palpable. Software sales reps were no different than used car salesman. We peddled our wares, did lunch, and were all lazy as hell.

"You don't go any further than me. I own the budget and control everything for Nano. You only meet with Sean. Anything you want to do, you have to run it by Sean first. And if Sean thinks it is worthwhile, he will put together a business case and run it past Nick. If Nick thinks it is worthwhile, he'll then put another business case together and raise it up to me. If I think it is worthwhile, then I'll raise that up with Randy (Global CIO). Randy doesn't make any decisions. I make all the decisions. Do you understand? And if you try to go around me, I'll have you removed as our sales rep. Do I make myself clear?"

This was going to be interesting. John was turning red as he finished his monologue. It was so well done that I'm sure he must have given that speech a thousand times to different sales reps. Inside, I was grinning from ear to ear.

This is why. The absolute worst thing for a sales rep is to waste his or her time. You have a limited amount of time – a year, a quarter, a month, or a week – to go close your deal and bring home the bacon. It is counterintuitive but nice customers are the worst to deal with. Nice customers treat you well and are courteous, but they can also waste your time. Nice customers have a tough time telling you the cold, hard facts that a deal can't get done or something can't happen in the timeframe in which you need it. Customers who are jerks have no issues with telling you the bad news up front.

The best sales reps I have ever met all say the same thing. They would prefer to deal with a jerk who can get a deal done than a nice customer who can't get anything done. This was the situation I was dealing with. Both Nick and John were jerks, but at least now I knew where I stood and how to deal with them. I could put the right strategies in place to neutralize them and get my deal done.

The mosaic was slowly starting to come together. I was going to have to create a little chaos internally to get the resources and momentum I needed. I was going to have to blow some things up at BUC and be disruptive to get the executives at the bank to look at the cloud the right way. Besides a customer signing ceremony, this is one of my favorite parts in a deal. It's the beginning and things are starting to come together. You are making your plans and getting the troops ready to go to war. In a few months, we would land on the beaches at Normandy. Game on.

CHAPTER 11

The Southern Gentleman

The last time anyone at Nano Canada met with Randal Snipes was two years ago. Known as Randy to everyone at the bank, he was a true southern gentleman. Randy was the Global CIO and EVP at BUC. Prior to BUC, Randy had spent a decade at Citigroup. He had worked his way up and eventually become the COO. Randy was truly a big fish in a big pond. He ran with the big dogs and could be found lunching with Jamie Dimon or briefing Sandy Weill. Somewhere along the way, there was a coup d'état and he found himself on the wrong side. That's how he landed at BUC. BUC's CEO realized that they needed a big fish to help guide them through the bank's next level of transformation. Randy's calm demeanor and collaborative leadership style were a perfect fit for the bank. He and his wife still had a sprawling mansion in Atlanta, rumored to be next to Elton John's, but they called their condo at the Ritz-Carlton in downtown Toronto home for the next few years.

I was stuck between a rock and a hard place. If I listened to Nick or John at BUC, I would never, ever get to see Randy. They would put up so many hurdles that even the best Olympic track and field stars would find it difficult to overcome. Two years ago, the President of Nano Canada had met with Randy and it had turned into a shit show. Our president had acted like a true used car salesman and tried to hawk a year-end licensing deal. He was abruptly kicked out after 15 minutes. I thought about it for a few minutes and knew that there was only one path forward. It was show time.

I had done a lot of research on Randy. I knew that when he was working at Citi, he also had a house in Southern Illinois and spent a fair amount of time there, commuting to New York. Randy loved blues music and had an impressive guitar collection. Going back to first principles, I thought, if you wanted to connect and talk to someone, what would you do? You would just reach out to them. Forrest Gump genius, right? So, I sat at my desk and wrote him a basic email. I said that I was the new Client Director responsible for the Nano/BUC relationship. I said that we had a lot in common as I had just moved up from Chicago, where I had lived for the last decade. I then called his office and left him a voicemail. Later that day, I got an email response saying that he would love to meet up. My heart started to race and my hands started to clam up. I was going to see the Global CIO at BUC. I was starting to get nervous. Don't mess this up, Trong. Like Hamilton in the musical, "I'm not throwing away my shot!"

Colleen Reid was Randy's trusted executive assistant. After Randy's email, I called her and we set up an appointment for me to meet with Randy. I really liked Colleen. She was smart, witty, and very well-read. She took great pride in her work, and it showed. I made small chitchat with Colleen and found out that she had grown up in Toronto and had an affection for Chinese food, especially dim sum. A woman after my own heart.

A week later.

I waited nervously in the reception area. Life comes down to just a handful of critical moments and this was one of them. If I blew it, I was assured a short career at Nano Canada.

"Randy will see you now," said Colleen as she guided me to Randy's office. I followed her obediently into Randy's corner office. He had a great view of the Toronto skyline. I extended my hand and nervously shook his. I kicked off the conversation.

"Randy, thanks for taking the time to see me today. I think there is a lot we can do together. I'd like to take the

relationship between our two companies to the next level."
Volley and set.

Randy looked at me with genuinely puzzled eyes.

"Trong, I'm not sure what you are talking about, but what relationship do you think we have between our two companies? As far as I know, it is nonexistent." Damn. He just spiked me. Time to pivot.

"Randy, you know, there are a lot of things Nano can do to help BUC reduce operational costs. For example, I know you have a massive outsourcing contract with IBM. What are you spending with them? Three, four hundred million? I think you are in year four of your contract. By now you are probably feeling a lot of pain with change requests. I know, because I used to write those contracts for IBM. Nickeling and diming is an Olympic sport at IBM."

I thought I might have struck a nerve, because he winced. Perfect. When you see a piece of string, start pulling on it. I dug a little deeper into my IBM experiences and what we used to do with customers in massive outsourced contracts. Slowly the conversation started to turn around. Randy was warming up.

I told Randy that I thought we could really transform BUC by having them move to the cloud. All of the data centers that they were running on-site, as well as the ones that were outsourced to IBM, were costing them a fortune.

I also told Randy that he would inevitably have to change some of his leadership team. I had met with most of them by now and a lot of them were dead weight. They clung to the past like it was their last breath. With that kind of legacy thinking, you really couldn't move forward. Randy liked my idea about the cloud but didn't say much when I talked about his leadership team. One thing he did admit to was that the bank moved as "slow as molasses." He was going to try and change that by breaking down the silos and fiefdoms that existed. I told him I was all in to help him do that.

A few hours after I left Randy's office, the shit definitely hit the proverbial fan. It got around that I had just met with Randy. Nick and John were on the warpath. How dare I go see Randy without their permission? Their executive assistants summoned me to their offices immediately. They were going to show me who was the boss and it definitely wasn't me. Little did they know that the news was about to get worse. Not only had I met Randy without their permission, but the meeting had gone so well that Randy asked me to set up monthly one-on-ones with him. Kaboom. I had just blown the shit up.

CHAPTER 12

David vs. Goliath (Part One)

Besides Chris Rock, the thing that makes me laugh the most is when I'm with customers and we talk about licensing. For those of you not in high tech or the software industry, licensing is when a high-tech company such as Nano sells its software for companies to use. The license is the proof of purchase and the mechanism that allows you to use the software. With it come many privileges and obligations. The license can be sold in different forms: you can have an annual license, a per-user license, an enterprise-wide license, and even a perpetual license that never expires. As you can see by this short explanation, the complexity can grow exponentially. I hear a lot from customers that our licensing is too complex and that we would be better served if we simplified it.

This is when I put on my best game face, pause to feign reflection, and empathize enough to make Oprah proud.

"I totally agree with you. It's so complex that I can't understand it myself. Let me raise this up as an issue with the leadership team to deal with and try to fix."

It's all true and I do raise the issue with our leadership team. However, this exercise is like waiting for Godot or chasing windmills. The following year, we actually make it even more complex. Our licensing practices are purposely designed to be complex. The main goal of the licensing and product teams is to extract as much money from our customers as possible, so they will find every nook, cranny, and angle to get the last dollar they can. It's not an accident that as soon as people start to understand our licensing practices and find loopholes, we instantly change them so that we have the upper hand.

There is one mistake most large companies make that they don't even realize. They think licensing and managing these licenses is an easy job. With that perspective, they usually put a junior person in charge of this function. They will hire someone who is a few years out of college to work with our licensing experts.

Look at it this way: you've got someone making $40K – $60K per year who barely knows what they are doing, going up against someone who is highly skilled, seasoned, and making $200K – $400K per year, with the same job function. The battle is over before it starts. It's like putting a great varsity athlete against Michael Jordan or LeBron James. It's not even fair. My peers and I think it is pretty obvious, but apparently it's not, because most of the time we end up working with customer licensing analysts who are barely out of college. When that happens, we know it is going to be a good year. Another quota blown out of the water.

Bhopinder Dohil was the licensing specialist assigned to BUC. His friends called him Bobby. I always liked hanging around Bobby because he made me laugh. It was always an interesting experience. Being a licensing specialist is the worst job in the world. If your job in life was to watch paint dry, his would be ten times worse. Bobby spends all day keeping up with the inane contractual terms that our product and legal teams come up with.

Then he uses that knowledge and builds licensing models for our customers. He is a complete Excel Jedi at this task. From there, he hops on conference calls or attends customer meetings, explaining the minutiae to our customers. I know we pay him a lot of money, but he has to do this for 14–16 hours a day, every day. And he does it with such style and grace. That's what I admire about him. He loves his craft the way Enzo Ferrari loves his cars.

Bobby and I became good friends. Whenever I needed any modeling or scenarios on how we should structure a deal, no matter how tired he was, Bobby always stepped up his game and gave me exactly what I needed. It would be safe to say that without Bobby, we really wouldn't have good deal structures or make it a win-win situation for our customers.

CHAPTER 13

The Bane Of My Existence

In the Batman comic book and movie, Bane is this terrifying and utterly vicious villain who ends up breaking Batman's back. He is supersized, has super strength, and is manically driven by his deprived background. Juiced by experimental drugs that made him what he is today, Bane manhandles Batman like a rag doll and ultimately breaks his back so that Bruce Wayne has to retire the mask and cape. The best and most expensive doctors in Gotham aren't going to be able to heal Bruce any faster. After all, he's just a man with a mask and will have to do physio like the rest of us.

"Trong, you are screwed!"

That was the refrain I heard from everybody. I had heard stories about Wendel Williams as soon as I arrived in Toronto. Wendel had been with the bank for 20 years. He and his team were technically in asset management but had negotiated every Nano contract since its inception. Contract negotiations are usually done by the procurement team. Arguably he knew more about Nano licensing terms and conditions than we did. Wendel had a well-earned reputation for keeping every sales rep and the company they represented in line. He negotiated the best contracts in Canada and you couldn't pull anything over on him. He was that good, that detailed, and that relentless. Wendel was going to be my Bane.

Bobby and I had an appointment to see Wendel and his team at BUC's Scarborough campus. We had a licensing contract renewal that we had to negotiate. For my management team, I laid it on pretty thick.

"This is hard stuff. Contract renewals are really tough and complicated. Tens and hundreds of millions of dollars are at risk. If we don't negotiate the right terms and conditions, the company could be at huge risk. Enterprise agreement renewals need to be highly rewarded and lucrative for the sales rep because they are so hard to do."

I'll let you in on a trade secret. Enterprise Agreement renewals are simple and easy. They aren't hard at all. Let me lay it out for you. Big enterprise customers that are on licensing subscription agreements with software companies like Nano have very little choice. They can threaten to move off your software, but that threat has a very low probability. The cost of them switching software once they are on a platform is so high that they might as well try to sell ice to Eskimos in January. It's not going to happen.

We call it a negotiation, but it's really not. The terms and conditions are already set, so there isn't that much negotiation in those areas. It's just an exercise in price times quantity. That's it. It's that simple. Sales reps just make it sound complicated because that's how we get paid. The more complicated and hard something seems, the easier it is for us to justify exorbitant commissions. God, I love playing that game. Did I tell you that negotiating enterprise license agreements is really hard?

We checked into security at BUC's Scarborough campus. We were in the building where they housed one of their major data centers and their call center. It was old, dark, and depressing. It was totally the opposite of the plush, bright, open splendor that can be found in their downtown offices. We sat around an oval conference table and made small talk with a few folks from his team. Five minutes later, Wendel strolled in and started scanning the room.

In the left corner, we have Trong Nguyen. Weighing 130 lbs. soaking wet and standing barely 5'4", our contender looks like a deer in the headlights as he jabs in the air at an imaginary opponent. In the right corner, we have Wendel

Williams standing at 6'7", and muscles shredded as Atlas' muscles must have been while holding the world on his shoulders. He's pointing one finger in the air. The crowd goes wild. What does that mean? Is he going to take Trong down in one second? One minute? What the hell does he mean?

Everyone was right. I'm screwed. Trong, get your shit together. Focus!

"So, you're the new sales rep from Nano. Let me lay the ground rules here. First, I want to know who you are visiting at BUC every week. I want a list of who you are seeing and what you will be talking about. I want that list sent to me every morning. If I ever find out that you met with a BUC executive without me knowing about it, I will make sure that is the last time you ever visit us again. Do I make myself clear?"

Drone launched. Wendel didn't flinch or pause as he felt me out.

"Wendel, I don't think that's how it works. I work for Nano and I work for Randy Snipes, your Global CIO. I don't work for you. If that's how you and BUC want to operate, I'm happy to comply, but I want an email directly from Randy copying his boss stating that fact. When I get that email, I'll be happy to execute on that. Do I make myself clear?"

Drone down. I said it with the confidence of a Navy Seal on a special ops mission. Time for another attack.

"Instead of wasting time to see who is the alpha, why don't we get down to business and discuss the licensing renewal?"

Without missing a beat, Wendel jumped in.

"Well, we were thinking of dropping your software. There are better alternatives from Cisco and Google. They have some great productivity and communications tools that we are piloting right now. I think we are probably going down that path, unless you guys can offer us an attractive deal."

Got it. So that's how he wants to play it.

"Wendel, you and BUC have the best deal in the country. I know you know that. Our software is world class and Gartner says so in their magic quadrant. Having said that, every customer is free to do whatever they think is best for their business. If that is the path you and BUC want to go down, then we are happy to start an audit. This audit will make sure we have the proper counts for your final true up and payment to us. Who on your team can I work with to start the audit?"

Second drone down. This was going to be fun.

"Well, I think that may be a bit premature. Why don't we have a follow-up meeting to discuss this a bit more next week? I'm sure there is something we can work out."

Wendel was now warming up.

With that, Bobby and I stood up and shook everyone's hands and left. In the parking lot, I smiled that victorious smile and said confidently to Bobby, "Dude, that's how we do it. Don't mess with the yellow man!"

I could tell he was impressed. Once I got in my BMW, I let out a big exhalation. God, I can't believe I faked and survived that. I was starting to shake a bit and looked down at my pants. It was hard to tell, but I think they were wet. Thirty minutes into my drive home, Wendel called my cell phone. I was pleasantly surprised. He said they had a 5% growth rate from the prior year. I told him I understood and thanked him for his candor.

For the next four months, we carried on the same pattern. It was like two gladiators going at it in the forum. Block, parry, strike. This was hard work. We had cheerleaders on both teams. And they cheered loudly too. Afterwards, Wendel and I would always carry on with our offline conversations. We talked candidly and worked the mechanics and details on how we could actually get a deal done and what would make sense for our different companies.

After six months, we finally got our license renewal done. We ended up exactly where we thought we would on that first day we met, but we had to put on a good show for our respective management teams. When it was finally signed, everyone was high-fiving each other. Both companies were declaring victories and savings. It was an amazing partnership.

CHAPTER 14

Sensei Mike

Karate was first practiced by people in Okinawa, an island off the coast of Japan, in the 17th century. The word literally means "the way of the empty hand." It is believed to have originated when kung fu masters from China shared some of the basic techniques with the people of the island. At the time, the Samurai ruling class had outlawed the use of weapons, and as a result these self-defense techniques became popular and quickly gained a following. With time, legitimate karate masters came into their own and different branches and styles developed. The most popular styles include Shotokan and Goju-Ryu. By the 20th century, karate had become a popular sport and was practiced by millions of people all over the world.

By now, I had been back in Toronto for eight months. I had closed the largest license renewal deal in the country. I was a hero and relished every minute of it. I was living the life and dining in different restaurants every night with customers on the company's dime. It couldn't get much better than this. I was living large. Literally.

I had lived this lifestyle in my twenties and thirties and when you are young, your body bounces back quickly. Now in my forties, I was starting to feel it. The economic wisdom that "there is no such thing as a free lunch" is so accurate. Everyone pays the piper; it's just a matter of when.

Sadly, the piper came knocking at my door and his name was Metabolism. And Metabolism was looking for payment in full. With all the drinking and eating out, I had put on 25 lbs. When your baseline weight is only 130 lbs, that percentage increase is enormous. And to top it off, I was feeling bloated and unattractive. To keep my alertness level up, I began to drink more and more coffee. I think I was up to 16 cups a day now. Damn. Something needed to change.

As an Asian, I always like to propagate the myths just to mess with people. Everyone thinks that I can rattle numbers off faster than Rain Man and can kill two flies at the same time with a pair of chopsticks, even though they are in different rooms. I taught Keanu Reeves how to do all the tight moves you saw in *The Matrix* movies. That's how I accidentally came to take up karate.

I decided I needed to do something physical to get back into shape. My only options were late at night, because I was out of the house every day by 6:15 am and the earliest I ever got home was 7 pm. I checked out a few dojos in the neighborhood. I talked to the masters to get a feel for each place. None of them really appealed to me until the last one. Like the best things in life, it was love at first sight.

Sensei Mike was a sixth-degree black belt. It's a monumental task just to get your black belt – first degree. To get your sixth degree, it means you are a master of masters. You devote your entire life to the art. And Sensei Mike was only 35. That means he had a God-given gift and probably started training when he was barely out of diapers. I had no doubt that Sensei Mike could maim people with just one hand and kill two flies with just one chopstick.

As I talked to Sensei, he told me that he had survived a tough childhood. He had grown up on the wrong side of the street and spent his days fighting kids throughout puberty. Then one day, as a teenager, he found karate. Young grasshopper Mike was particularly adept at sparring, so he started entering tournaments and won most of them.

Sensei also had another unique talent. He could learn any kata after going through it only once. A kata is a series of punches, kicks, and movements that mimic fighting real opponents. To advance in karate and get your higher belts, you need to practice and execute your katas to perfection. To give you a sense of how hard that is, picture this. It is equivalent to an author writing a New York Times bestseller with only one draft. We all know that's near impossible, but Sensei Mike could do it. I signed up and couldn't wait to start this new journey of enlightenment.

Ichi, ni, san, shi. Push-ups, sit-ups, burpees, squats, and army crawl. Run. Stop. Run the other way. It was relentless. I thought I was going to die. I was gasping for air like a 95-year-old on his deathbed. I saw my life flash before me and knew my time was up. I was going to die, and it wasn't from some punk on the streets of New York or some stray bullet from a fire fight. It was going to be from the instructor in my karate class.

During one of my gasps for dear life, I looked around and saw that everyone was smiling and talking about the great day they had had in school. The only one drenched in sweat and dying was me. Everyone looked like they had just come back from a leisurely stroll. Damn. After the warm-up, Sensei came out and started teaching the class. Sensei pulled me aside and started teaching me the basics of kicking and punching. That night, I went home sore and bruised, embarrassed and dejected because I was humbled by 14-year-olds. They had pushed me to my limit, but I didn't break. I would be back the next night for more.

CHAPTER 15

My Dark Secret

As the months went by, I got to know Randy's assistant, Colleen, a lot better. Occasionally we would go out to dinner and scope out the best Chinese restaurants. We ordered enough food for five people and sampled everything that looked delish. Then I would send the rest home with her for leftovers. At dinner, we discussed books we'd read, smart shows we'd watched, and more importantly I just spent time picking her brain. I sought her advice and guidance on how to deal with different situations and people within the bank.

On the surface, you would never have expected an executive assistant to be my mentor. But candidly, she was the best consigliere I ever had. What made Colleen special was that she was wickedly smart and devoutly loyal to her boss. She played mother hen and made sure Randy's interests were always looked after. Colleen knew I wanted the same thing, so from that perspective, we were always aligned. Not everyone on Randy's team saw eye-to-eye with his direction or strategy. They would quietly talk behind his back and plot to undermine him. Fortunately, Colleen was a better forensic scientist than Sherlock Holmes. In her own unique way and via back channels, Colleen got to the root of things fairly quickly. She diffused and neutralized situations before they had a chance to get out of hand.

My peers always took the most valued executives they worked with out on special occasions. I always went the other way and invited their executive assistants. They are really the unsung heroes. They were worth their weight in gold and I was going to treat them as such. It was three weeks before Christmas and I invited all of the executive assistants of the top executives that I dealt with at BUC to a Christmas luncheon. We made reservations at the Ritz-Carlton and I came prepared with goodie bags. They were filled with Tim Horton gift cards, David's Tea trinkets, good-smelling soap from The Body Shop and a few pieces of delicious Swiss chocolate. They came with a personalized note and wrapped in a baby blue ribbon.

Over appetizers, the main course, and too many bottles of sauvignon blanc, we solved most of the world's problems. By the time lunch was done at 3:30 pm, we had solved world hunger, figured out how to shuttle entire colonies to Mars, and how Bill Clinton smoked pot without actually inhaling it. It was tricky, but we wrote mathematical proofs to back up our assertions.

No matter who you're entertaining, one of the things you need to learn how to do in sales is drink. It's a practice as old as time. When Genghis Khan wanted to expand his region and territories, he would assemble his generals and they would drink and feast. Genghis would sell them his vision of building this great empire. They would toast to conquered lands, trash talk about the Chinese and Merkits and, when sufficiently liquored, they pledged in blood to support the agreed-upon expansion plans. Genghis always made sure that everyone knew he was the MAN. No one outdrank him. The next day, all the generals would go and repeat the same process with their officers and enlisted men. Fast-forward 800 years and nothing has really changed.

Genghis now goes by the title of CEO, generals are called account executives, and soldiers are the core and extended sales teams. Alcohol has many benefits, but the most useful is that it helps to lower people's inhibitions. When you drink enough, the dopamine kicks in, and you become happy and relaxed. In that state, you are more open to suggestions and ideas. That's why sales reps love taking their customers out to eat and drink.

When a customer's guard is sufficiently lowered by alcohol, they are more open to suggestions of buying what you are peddling. But here's the gotcha with alcohol – it is indiscriminate. It treats everyone the same. The key for sales reps is that they need to be able to handle their alcohol. They need to be able to drink with their customers and still be coherent enough to guide the conversation and remember everything that is discussed. That's why most sales reps are professional drinkers.

When I first started going out with other reps to practice our calling as salesmen, I quickly learned that drinking was a mandatory Olympic sport. The guy or gal that could outdrink everyone and still function the next day won the gold medal. These sessions were always fun, but I had a dark secret. A secret that was so bad it would end my career if it ever got out: I can't hold my liquor. I'm not ashamed to admit it – I'm a lightweight when it comes to drinking.

Not to get defensive, but there are legitimate reasons why I can't hold my alcohol. First, it's about biology and physics. When you weigh only 130 lbs. soaking wet, you have very little body mass to absorb the alcohol. Someone who weighs 180–220 lbs. will always have a competitive advantage. The second is that I'm Asian. There, I'm going to play the race card. Everyone knows that we have a defective gene that doesn't allow us to process alcohol very well. That's why we turn beet red when we drink. Google that, it's true!

So how do I cope and make sure that no one finds out my secret? I do what women have been doing since the beginning of time. I fake it. I drink only half of my drink and then order another one. I take my beer with me to the washroom and dump three quarters of it in the urinal and come back with an almost empty glass. And if I am feeling especially deviant, I go to the restaurant ahead of time and give the waitress an extra-large tip not to put any alcohol in my gin and tonic. I'd just hung out with six fabulous executive assistants drinking way too much during a workday. Full disclosure, I did go to the restaurant 15 minutes early and had a discrete conversation with the waitress. As far as I know, my secret is still safe. I can drink with the best of them…

CHAPTER 16

Selling Hope

Billy Graham, Jerry Falwell, Jim Bakker: all of these religious men had something in common. They could sell. As a kid, I used to love watching them preach on Sunday mornings or study their re-runs in syndication. The emotional rollercoaster they would take you on in 42 minutes would bring you to tears – literally. They would all start the same way. They welcomed and brought you into their family. It was inclusion before inclusion became popular. Then they would identify one problem that we as a society should think about.

This problem, when unmanaged, would lead one to spiral out of control. And truth be told, none of us wanted to be out of control. Now everyone was nervous and sweating with anticipation. How were we going to fix this problem? We sat in rapture. Then Billy, Jerry, and Jim would pause and pivot. They continued with a few words of encouragement. They would plant the seeds for a solution. With a lot of hard work and practice we just might be able to find redemption. Whatever our transgressions – infidelity, substance abuse, breaking one of the ten commandments – there was hope. They would help us through our particular shortcomings. By the time the show was over, we felt good about ourselves. We had hope that we could fix our problems if we came back the following week.

The average sales rep at Nano thought that we were in the software or technology business. That's why they were average. We were no different than the Sunday televangelists. We were in the business of selling hope. It just so happened that the tool we used to implement that hope was technology. Kevin Lemire was Randy's right-hand man and his chief of staff. Randy was grooming Kevin to be his successor. Trained as an accountant, Kevin was on an even keel and balanced. He took a very methodical approach to everything. Politics were all around him, but he never joined in. He treated it all as just noise. Kevin always favored the best and most logical ideas.

"Kevin, here's what I'd like to do. You guys are going to the Valley anyway to meet up with VCs and other tech companies. Why don't you spend a day at Nano? I don't want us to talk about technology. BUC is going through a major transformation. You guys were lucky that 2008 didn't have a material impact on you. Nano went through a major transformation when we went from a software to a services company. There are a lot of great lessons learned that BUC executives could get out of this session."

There it was – hope.

"I'll have our top leaders in marketing, HR, finance, and strategy walk you through how we approached our predicament and transformed the company. There are a lot of lessons there that are applicable to BUC."

Hook, line, and sinker. I was reeling it in. Kevin was Spock-like in his predictability. He thought it was a great idea.

"Can you help me put an agenda together?"

"Of course. Let me have my team pull something together and I'll get it to you later this week. Is that ok in terms of timing?"

"Perfect. Thanks, Trong. Let's make this happen."

Putting together an executive briefing is like the Dell build-to-order model in its glory days in the 1990s. There's the illusion and the reality. Dell has mastered this sleight of hand. Here's how it works. Dell's tagline has always been that you can build your PC and have it your way. The Dell guy, when he wasn't smoking up, could attest to the model's flexibility. I'm going to let you in on a secret. Here's how it actually works behind the scenes. Dell makes it look like you have all these options and configuration items. But when you net it out, you can only customize two or three options. That's how they were able to get scale and efficiency. We ran our executive briefings the same way.

A week later.

"Kevin, so here's what my team put together. The list is pretty long. We have around 50 modules to choose from."

"Wow. That seems pretty daunting."

"Kevin, let me do this. Why don't I take a stab at putting this briefing together? We'll narrow it down to five modules. With breaks and lunch, that will take us the whole day."

Two days later.

"So, here's what the five modules look like. We start at 7:30 am and end at 5:30 pm followed by dinner at this fantastic seafood restaurant."

"Thank you. That's perfect. Let's lock down the agenda. I'll circulate it to the other executives."

Michael Dell would have been proud. I had applied his business model in a totally different context.

CHAPTER 17

Passive–Aggressive

When you ask the average sports fan what made Michael Jordan great, they usually give a superficial response. He was a great defender. He had an amazing dunk. He could float in the air. They weren't wrong, but they weren't right either. Michael had some amazing physical talents, but what made him great were his drive and work ethic. Before the 1991 season, the Chicago Bulls had never won a championship. Michael still had the physical talents and dominated when he was on the court, but he was outplayed and overshadowed by Isaiah, Magic, and Larry. Tired of losing, Michael changed his approach in 1991. He decided to put the team first. Instead of individual accolades, he would look to make every member of his team better by amplifying their natural talents. And that's how he won his first championship.

Syam Adusumilli was our Michael Jordan. He was bald and brown as a chestnut and he did whatever it took to make the team successful. And that's how our team won. Syam was a veteran of the tech industry. He was an engineer by training and had spent over a decade at IBM. His formal title was Industry Marketing Manager, but his job description was more of a handyman. He did anything and everything the team needed to help us win.

Most customers don't realize that putting together a great executive briefing takes an inordinate amount of work. It takes months and months of planning and preparation. We put together briefing documents for the speakers, customer executives, and our own leadership team. We have prep calls with each of them multiple times, just to make sure that everyone is aligned. And if we do it right, we'll make it look as easy as Michael hanging in the air for two minutes and then dunking.

I had delegated the task of putting the BUC executive briefing together to Syam. What made this task difficult was that the application we used to put the briefing together wasn't really an application. It was more like an Excel spreadsheet on an old PC under someone's desk at the briefing center. It was held together by a few Band-Aids and Excel macros. I was amazed the first time I saw it. It was akin to communication in the 1800s. If you wanted to send a message, you either sent pigeons or a legion on a ship and hoped that the message got there within six months to a year. You would never have thought that we worked for a software company. Like a true champ,

Syam didn't complain or ask, "Why me?" He just smiled and said, "Ok."

Everyone flew in the night before. We had an amazing list of speakers. We managed to twist arms and cajole our top executives in strategy, human resources, and marketing to attend and speak to the top executives at BUC. The list of executives attending from BUC was just as impressive. True to his word, Randy had invited his peers and some of his direct reports who would have a huge impact on Nano's business. I was especially looking forward to spending some time with John Thompson, SVP of Data Center and Operations, and hopefully building a better relationship with him. Syam had arranged for a car service for all of us. Randy and I had our own limo that we would ride in together. The others would take different limos.

I was in our limo with Randy and we were talking about the beautiful weather and the agenda for the day. We were looking forward to a great day of sessions and learning from each other. His phone rang unexpectedly. It was only 7:30 am PDT. Must be someone from Toronto. It was a female voice. Either Colleen or one of the other admins. Randy listened for a minute.

"He can't find anyone else to cover for him?" He listened for another 30 seconds. "OK." He hung up.

"What's up?" I asked.

"John Thompson is not coming. Apparently, some data center issue. Servers went down and he has to stay back to make sure they get them back up."

I let that sink in for a second. Servers in data centers go down all the time. That's just the nature of technology. If John didn't have people who could fix and address those issues, then he shouldn't be in his job. Then it dawned on me. He just didn't want to come out for the Nano executive briefing. It was cowardly of him to tell us at the last minute and make a lame excuse on top of that.

"Passive–aggressive." I stated.

"Looks like it."

I looked at Randy and he just sat there. He was starting to turn red. I had never seen Randy like this before. I could tell he was trying his best to keep composure. He wasn't saying anything, but I knew what he was thinking inside: "John Thompson is a jerk. You want to mess with me? Let's do this!" We rode in silence for the next five minutes. I knew better than to say anything. I just sat there in complete and utter silence.

When we got to the executive briefing center, I guided everyone to our designated room. Out of all the companies that I have worked for, Nano is definitely the best at hosting briefings. Their briefing center is a palace. It screams of money but in a subtle way. It tells everyone who visits that we know what we are doing. You can put your trust in us and in return we will make you just as successful as we are. It even has its own highly skilled barista who can make you any variety of coffee from any part of the world.

The first session was a screaming success. Syam was able to snag John Hanby, our EVP of corporate strategy to give a talk about how Nano changed its corporate strategy to morph from a software company into a services company. Make a note: when you are putting together an executive briefing, make sure you vet your speakers thoroughly and carefully. Your customers are spending a day or two to fly to your corporate headquarters. Usually there will be a group of them. They are making a massive commitment of time and money to be there. Make sure you show up with the best of what your company has to offer.

John got up in front of the room. He walked through his last 15 years at Nano as background and context. He talked about his sabbatical over the last three years to help the Obama administration change healthcare in the US as its Chief Technology Officer. John had game. No one was going to argue that. John had 80 slides, but over the next 60 minutes he didn't use one of them. He was Warren Buffet and Charlie Munger all rolled into one. He was holding court like they always do at their annual Berkshire shareholders' meeting. By the time John was done, I thought the executives from BUC were going to jump up and scream in excitement. It wouldn't have surprised me if they had asked for his autograph. We knew we had nailed it after John left. He set the tone for the day and everyone who followed benefited from his halo effect.

Running an executive briefing is like cooking. You get excited because you can create so many wonderful tastes and flavors for your customers. But you can definitely overdo it. The trick is to have just the right number of sessions and schedule enough breaks and free time. The breaks are your seasoning and spices. Under or overdo it and you've just ruined a great meal. Over dinner, we got to know each of the executives on a personal level. We asked them about their families, hobbies, and more importantly what made them laugh – because ultimately that's how you touch their soul.

I sat next to Randy. He ordered the baked salmon. I ordered a Flintstone-sized bone-in ribeye.

"Trong, this was a wonderful day. Thanks so much for pulling this together for my team. I know what we need to do next. Can you help us get to the cloud?"

Is a poutine a day good for you? Should the Colonel put more than 20 pieces of chicken in his bucket? Is bacon a vegetable? Hell yeah!

"Of course. I'd be happy to help with that."

CHAPTER 18

Request For Proposal

Most software companies work the same way – SAP, Oracle, Microsoft, Salesforce. They have a team of sales reps who sell the software, also known as licensing. And then they have a stepchild of an organization called services. The services team's responsibility is to sell implementation services to help install the software and get it running properly. The software sales reps get paid on the annual contract value (ACV) of the licensing part of the deal. The software sales reps don't get paid on the services component, so for all intents and purposes, it is an afterthought. And if they do get paid on it, it is usually such a small bonus that they don't really care. Nano was no different.

You can win a lot of new customers and close some amazing deals by just focusing on the software. If you want to be relevant and truly add value to a customer, you need to focus on the overall solution. An overall solution encompasses both software and services. For the average sales rep, this is really hard to do. Not because they don't know how, but because it goes against everything that they have ever been taught. Sales reps, from the day they were born, have always been taught that you make money by working the compensation plan. If you don't get paid on it, you don't sell it. So now you are in the unenviable position of telling them that everything they have ever been taught is just not good practice. It's akin to telling a six-year-old that Santa doesn't really exist. That just can't be true.

The first time I met Vincent Presley, I had to do a double take. I was expecting some white guy – a WASP of European descent. Vincent was a dark brown Indian dude. Judging by his skin tone, I'm guessing he was from Sri Lanka or somewhere in southeast Asia. I made a mental note: over beers one day, I was going to have to ask him about his name. I know for a fact that Presleys are not indigenous to Kerala or Chennai.

Vincent was the delivery executive assigned to Nano. He owned our services approach and how we would deliver solutions to BUC. We grabbed coffee to get to know each other better. After five minutes with Vincent, I liked him right away. He was smart, articulate, and wanted to make a difference. He was in the process of doing his Executive

MBA at Queen's University, so he was burning the candle at both ends. I didn't realize this then, but I had completely lucked out. Apparently, most of the other delivery executives weren't that good. In Vincent, I found a kindred spirit. He wasn't afraid to question authority or the status quo and was always looking at different angles to make solutions work.

I pulled our whole team together to give them the marching orders. Three weeks after we came back from our executive briefing, BUC released a Request for Proposal (RFP) for a cloud solution. It was interesting that the first time I read it, it felt and smelt like a complete outsourcing solution. For those of you readers at home, an outsourcing solution is when a customer wants you to run and manage their programs (applications) in your data center. As the "outsourcer," you are responsible for everything. With an outsourcing solution, they still have the flexibility they had when they ran everything internally themselves, but someone else is responsible for it. Theoretically, outsourcing solutions are supposed to be cheaper than running the solution internally, because the outsourcer has economies of scale. They could use the same teams to manage multiple customers at the same time. In practice, though, it never worked out that way, because the outsourcer would nickel and dime you to death. What customers were paying for was really the flexibility of being able to staff up and down as business conditions dictated. Employees were now the outsourcer's problem, not theirs.

"Max, here's what I need you to do. Go through each section and give me your thoughts. Let me know how you think we should approach this."

"No problem. I got this."

"Vincent, here's what I need you to do. Pull our services team together and let me know how we can go about implementing this. I know we don't have a lot of expertise in Canada, so go to the US and get it. I know those guys have done lots of these implementations before."

"Trong, no problem. I'm on it."

As I was noodling on this, I knew what the exam question was going to be. We had to address the bank's security and audit requirements. If we couldn't address them adequately to pass the sniff test with the Canadian regulators (OSFI) and the US regulators (OCC), we were dead in the water.

This RFP was really about making sure that BUC was comfortable with our controls and processes. They, in turn, would then bring it up with the regulators and make them comfortable with our solution for the bank. Then OSFI and the OCC would bless our solution.

Responding to RFPs is a lot like competing in sports. The goal is to always stay in the game long enough so that eventually you will hit that home run or score the needed touch down. Both start the same way. First you feel each other out. That's the first quarter. You figure out who needs what. You run a few plays and see how the other team responds. Then you go on the attack. You tell the customer about your solution and why it would rock their world if they had it. That's the second quarter. The customer then comes back and tells you that they have other options. They don't need your solution. You go on the defense and make sure every man is covered. That's the third quarter. Then you blitzkrieg them with everything that you have. You agree on terms, you agree on pricing, you align your executives with theirs. That's the fourth quarter. You don't leave anything to chance. You don't take NO for an answer. You don't leave anything on the field. You close them.

That was essentially our plan to get this deal done. I told the guys to answer YES to everything in the RFP. We could do what they were looking for, but we had caveats and qualifiers with every answer. That way we could legitimately say that we could meet all of their requirements when it came to the Question and Answer sessions. When Max and Vincent were done, we had so many caveats that the lawyers were going to have a field day. We were going to keep them gainfully employed for years.

Nano had never done a cloud deal with a bank in Canada. There was no template to follow, because it had never been done before. We were breaking new ground and building the plane as we were flying it.

CHAPTER 19

Swimming In The Deep End

In the opening scene of Gladiator, you see Russell Crowe's character walking through the tall wheat fields. It is in slow motion. The music is haunting. You can feel a lifetime of anguish and pain in those few minutes as he caresses the wheat along his path. You know a lot of bad things have happened to him in the past; you just don't know what. It's the same feeling I get when I go to meet a new VP of procurement for the first time. I've been here before. I'm taking in the sun. I'm smelling the fresh air, because the next few breaths could be my last.

The relationship between sales reps and procurement professionals has historically been antagonistic. And understandably so. They are essentially two sides of the same coin. The role of the sales rep is to try to extract as much money from a customer as possible. The role of a procurement person is to try to save as much money for their company as possible. Hence the healthy tug of war. Every time I've been in a tough customer negotiation for a large complex deal, I feel like one of those gladiators fighting in the coliseum. You do your best, you try to trade blows, and you pray to God that you make it out alive.

"Hi Dave, I'm Trong. I'm your 6'4" devilishly handsome sales rep responsible for BUC."

I launch the first salvo with humor. Dave chuckles. That line is like bacon. It works every time. Dave Day was the new VP of procurement for BUC. I liked Dave a lot. He was easygoing, down-to-earth and very different from other procurement executives I've worked with before. He talked about partnership and win–win relationships. And the surprising part was that I could tell that he meant it. Dave was swimming in the deep end and he didn't even know it yet. Dave told me that I'd be working closely with his new team. There were a couple of new guys that he had brought over from a different area of the business. I loved it! I couldn't wait.

"Trong, I want to make sure we are clear on the rules of engagement here. You and your team are to only interface with my team during this RFP process. All questions are to be sent directly to us. We will pull all questions from the different vendors and send the responses out to everyone at the same time. If we find you talking to anyone else, we will disqualify you. We want to make sure this process is as fair as possible. Are we clear?"

"Sir, yes, sir!" I saluted.

I felt bad, but I had just straight-up lied to his face. Dave was a nice guy and he probably wasn't going to like me afterwards, but I knew what I had to do. When you are on the hunt and chasing the big whale, the last thing you want to do is follow orders from procurement. That's the fastest way to lose a deal.

By this time, Max and I were like two peas in a pod. We could finish each other's thoughts and sentences. Most of the time I didn't even have to say anything. I would give Max a look and he knew exactly what I wanted or what I was looking for. We put together a plan. It was so basic and simple. In other words, it was pure genius. Every day, we would meet with anyone from BUC that would meet with us. We would talk about what they wanted to talk about. Then, when we had about ten minutes of the meeting left, Max and I would do our one-two punch. Here's how I would tee it up for Max in a typical customer meeting:

"Mr. Customer, let me tell you about what we are doing at BUC with our cloud. There's real potential here to help transform the bank and make it into a true digital bank. Max, tell Mr. Customer what our cloud service does." And with that soft pitch, Max would swing like Babe Ruth. Thwack! It's out of the park. Another home run.

Within two weeks, the buzz was palpable. Everywhere we went, people were echoing everything we had been telling them. And they did it verbatim. It wasn't long before I got called into the principal's office.

"Trong, I thought I made it very clear to you when we talked a couple of weeks ago that you and your team were not to talk to anyone about the RFP. What am I missing here?"

"Dave, listen man, I don't know what you are talking about. I have these weekly and monthly meetings with everyone at BUC. I cover off our usual business. It's not my fault they are curious and start asking me questions about it. The issue is with the guys at BUC. If you don't want me meeting with anyone to cover the business stuff, I need that in writing from Randy, your Global CIO. I don't want anyone thinking I am not doing my job."

With that, Dave went quiet. I felt bad for Dave. He was such a nice guy. He just had no idea he was swimming in the deep end.

CHAPTER 20

The Valley Of Despair

Going through an RFP process is no different than dating. Everyone is putting their best foot forward to make themselves attractive for the other party. The customers tell you that their environment is very simple. There won't be a lot of integration issues. The vendors tell the customers that their solution works out of the box. There won't be a need for consulting or implementation services. We tell the other person what they want to hear. That way we can all be happy. At some point, when the honeymoon is over, reality sinks in and it looks a lot different than everyone thought.

Nano was invited to the finals presentation. This is where you put your BEST foot forward to try and convince the customer to go with your solution. You need to be in full courting mode. Max and I had been noodling on our strategy for a couple of weeks. We knew everyone was going to tell BUC how great their solution was and that they would have no issues whatever installing or using their software. While everyone was going to zig, we decided to zag.

"Good morning. Thank you for inviting us to the cloud RFP finals presentation. I want to walk you through what moving to the cloud with Nano is going to look like." I asked Max to go to the next slide. I pointed at the big dip in the chart.

"This happens with every one of our customers. First the implementation project goes well. Then we turn on the cloud service for the first test users. All hell breaks loose. Nothing works. This is what we call the valley of despair. This happens with every deployment."

For the next twenty minutes Max and I outlined in excruciating detail every issue that they were most likely to run into. We also talked about how we would address those issues and what BUC needed to do in order to prepare their organization for the eventual hiccups.

"Wait, are you telling us that we are going to have major implementation issues? You mean you can't guarantee that it will go smoothly?" asked one of the panelists.

"That's exactly what we are telling you. We've never had a project go smoothly before. We always run into the valley of despair, but we always get you out of it. The BUC implementation will be no different."

BUC was no different from any other customer that I have ever worked with. They appreciated our candor and honesty. While everyone else was telling them how great their service or solution was, we went completely the other way. We told them that moving to the cloud was like going to see your cardiologist. No one really wants to be there because the doctor tells you to curb your vices, exercise and adopt a healthy lifestyle. You know inherently that the doctor is right, but the medicine still tastes bad.

"We've decided that Nano's cloud solution is the right path to go. We'd like to start negotiations with you immediately. However, we do have a backup plan. We'll be negotiating with that vendor as well, just in case we can't come to terms with Nano. We just wanted to be completely transparent with you," Dave stated.

I had been training for this moment for the last 20 years – literally and figuratively. From a sales perspective, I had climbed my way up from hardware sales, software sales, and services sales. Now I was putting it all together and selling a cloud solution to a global bank. One day I would look back and tell my kids about this milestone moment. I felt like Michael Jordan in 1989.

I was getting giddy. I was at the top of my game and I was going to start negotiations with a child. I was starting to count my chickens, and damn, there were going to be lots of them. I could start supplying to Colonel Sanders.

"And we've retained outside counsel. You will be negotiating with Daniel Finkelstein. But of course, I'll be overseeing everything."

Shit! I was just about to tutor Dave and give him an MBA in enterprise negotiations when he decided that he was going to tutor and give me a PhD in humility. Smart. Very smart. My estimation of Dave just increased dramatically.

When you were a kid and you were petrified of stuff, no matter what it was, the feelings were the same. Spiders, snakes, or the grim reaper – they would all elicit the same physiological reaction. You feel like your heart is beating a lot faster than it should. Your hands get clammy. Beads of sweat start to form on the top of your head and slowly trickle down the side of your face. Your shoulders start to tighten. Then the hairs on the back of your neck stand up. They are so straight you would swear they were saluting you. Then the anxiety turns into pure panic. When anyone said Dan Finkelstein's name in the high-tech industry, that's exactly what happened.

Dan was the complete package. He graduated magna cum laude for his bachelor's degree and then went on to graduate top of his class at the University of Toronto's famed Faculty of Law. He was a partner at one of the most prestigious law firms in Canada. He charged $2,000 an hour for his services and was worth every penny. Dan focused on commercial law with a specialization in technology. Anytime a major corporation in Canada needed to negotiate an outsourcing or technology contract, they called Dan. He would bill them hundreds of thousands of dollars for his services and help them save millions of dollars. Dan was like Santa Claus at Christmas. Every one of his customers left with a smile.

"Dave, thanks for giving us this opportunity. I'm looking forward to working with Dan to get this deal done."

Over the next four weeks, we worked with Dan every day. We swapped legal papers back and forth. Redlines on the contract were fixed and then tweaked again. Dan was like an author finishing up his masterpiece. He anguished over every word and the structure of every sentence. I wouldn't admit this to anyone at Nano, but I really liked Dan. We were like fierce gladiators going at it. He was so good that he forced you to up your game. And in the process, he made everyone better. We quickly got through most of the business terms. We settled on price, we agreed upon the structure of the contract, and begrudgingly settled on limitations of liability. The one issue that we kept pushing back and forth on was audit rights. BUC wanted the ability to audit our data centers. They had this ability in all of their previous contracts and needed this clause to pass their regulatory requirements. This wasn't going to happen with our cloud service, so we kept on telling them NO.

When a customer is buying an outsourcing or cloud service, they are essentially depending on the vendor (like Nano) to run their back-end operations and infrastructure. They buy this as a service. The vendor tells BUC that they can provide this service for a set price. The vendor then delivers that service. Customers want the ability to check and make sure that the vendor is providing the services as advertised and agreed to in their contracts, either directly or using a third party. Hence, they wanted the "right to audit." Nano was not willing to provide this right because if we opened this can of worms for BUC, we would have to open it up to everyone. Nano was making a bet that our solution and price were so much better than those of the nearest competitor that customers would forgo these rights in order to get access to our service. And until now, we had been completely right.

CHAPTER 21

Help

December 21st, 2 pm.

Sean O'Reilly called me into his office. At this point in our relationship, we were comfortable and knew each other well enough that we usually just had short conversations multiple times a day. The fact that I was sitting in his office a few days before Christmas would make even the Dalai Lama antsy.

"Trong, I'm going to be honest with you. We want to do this deal with you, but I don't think we are going to be able to get it done. It's not about the price. We think we are getting a good deal. It's not about the solution. We think your solution is industry-leading. It's about the audit rights.

You know we are a bank. We are conservative by nature. Without audit rights, we can't do it."

Small beads of sweat started to form on my head. Never let them see you sweat. Shit. Too late. A drop started to roll down the side of my face.

"I want you to pull everyone together in a couple of days. I want your top executives in that meeting. We'll have all of the BUC executives there as well. I want your top decision makers in that room. We are either going to do this deal or not. If we aren't going to do it, let's just move on and stop wasting each other's time."

"Sean, OK. I hear the ask. I understand the ask. Let me see what I can do." I gulped. My shoulders started to tense. Breathe. Inhale. Exhale. Slowly. Do it again. I had no idea how I was going to do this. We were four days away from Christmas. It was our quarter end. All of the execs we needed were tied up in last-minute deals. And the ones that weren't tied up weren't the ones that we needed. I immediately launched missiles all over the place, hoping that one of them would land. Emails were going out faster than my panic attacks.

When you are staring death in the face, everything becomes crystal clear. All your pretenses, preconceived notions and priorities go out the window. For the longest time, I had made it look like I was king of the hill. I was a client director and ran a big sales team. And truth be told, according to me, sales drives everything at Nano. I made it look like another Oracle, IBM or Dell. In those organizations, sales *is* the king that drives everything. On my deathbed of driving this deal, I had to admit that I wasn't shit. Being a client director at Nano didn't mean squat. I was a glorified order taker. I might as well have been working for Apple. Product engineering drives everything at that company. They make all the decisions about what products to produce, how they are sold, and how much money they are going to allocate to the sales function just to keep the lights on.

With that clarity, I realized that my boss wasn't going to be able to help. Just like me, they were kings and emperors without any clothes. I needed to get to the VPs in engineering who ran the cloud service. They were the only ones who were going to be able to make decisions around engineering the service or agree to audit rights because they ran the cloud service.

Nathaniel Cameroon was a director on our cloud engineering team. His title belied his level of influence in the company. He had been at Nano for over a decade. An engineer and wordsmith by trade, he literally wrote every contract that Nano had ever had for customers who came on our cloud service. He was a Brit and carried himself the way that children of old money do. To bring himself down to our level, he insisted everyone just call him Nathan. It gave him a more pedestrian persona. What made Nathan so valuable to the cloud engineering team was that he was adept technically but could match that engineering prowess with the written language. He had the ability to wield the

Queen's English with the precision of a laser beam. I wrote to Nathan and his boss. In my email, I pleaded and begged for their help. I copied the entire world just to make sure my message did not get missed. I had hit the emergency button and was waiting for the cavalry to show up. Please come. We need help.

CHAPTER 22

The Ninth Inning

December 23rd, 4 pm.

At about 3:55 pm, everyone started to stroll into Nano's downtown office. We were fortunate that BUC's office was in the adjacent building. As the BUC executives were registering with our receptionist, I greeted them and shook their hands. Max was right there beside me as we formed the receiving line. This was the calm before the storm. We made small talk and slowly everyone sat down. True to Sean's word, he had all of BUC's top executives there. I panned the room and saw the Global CIO, Chief Information Security Officer, the Head of Risk, the Head of Audit, and the Head of Operations. On Nano's side, we had Max, myself, and our Director of Sales. On the phone, we also had a couple of our executives who weren't able to make it in person. Given our predicament, we did the only thing we could do. We set up a conference call so that they could participate remotely. It was not ideal, but beggars can't be choosers. That was strike one.

We went around the room and did quick introductions. Sean kicked off the meeting, explaining why we were all there and the intention of the meeting. Randy, usually the quiet and reserved one, finally spoke.

"Trong, we appreciate all your help to date. We need to decide if we are going to do this deal or not. We can't get past Risk and Audit on our side unless we have audit rights."

I nodded my head in agreement.

"So, who in this room or on the conference call can make that decision so we can either move forward or kill this project?"

Our Director of Sales in the room started chiming in. He did his best to dodge and deflect. He lobbed one up to our VP of Sales who was dialed into the conference line as well. He did his best to bob and weave. He employed every technique that we have ever learned in sales school. If there was a masterclass in dodging bullets or speaking without saying anything, he'd be teaching it. Unfortunately, we were dealing with the top executives at BUC. They were there for a reason and were really good at what they did. They saw through the smokescreen pretty quickly.

"It sounds to me like we don't have anyone in this meeting who can make a decision on audit rights. Frankly, we are a bit disappointed. We asked for your decision makers to be in this meeting so that we can come to consensus as to what we are going to do with this cloud deal." Randy had had enough. That was strike two.

Sean broke in. "Trong, you knew this was an important meeting. Why didn't you have the folks that could make the decisions here? I guess you guys are not serious about doing this deal." This was getting bad. Our biggest cheerleader was losing faith.

I looked at them, partially deflated, partially embarrassed, partially helpless. I had tried my best and come up short.

Our VP of Sales made one last-ditch effort. "Randy, I know you and your team are disappointed. It's not Trong or Max. They tried their best to pull this meeting together. Our Head of Engineering and Product Development was triple-booked and just couldn't make this time that you had set up. He's on another call dealing with major customer issues right now and trying to fix them."

I saw the pitch and decided to take another swing. "Our Head of Engineering is the only person that can make the decisions around audit rights and what you want to do. We are a couple of days away from Christmas. I know you are all breaking for a week. Can we set up a meeting for the first week of January when you come back? We'll have Nathan Cameroon here in person as well. He'll stay the week with us and we'll get through all the issues in real time."

The room went quiet. Everyone looked at Randy.

"OK. We'll have that meeting in the first week of January. If we can't resolve the issues in that meeting, we will have no choice but to go with Plan B."

With that, Randy closed his notebook. Everyone took his cue, stood up and walked out behind him. I was speechless. The count was three balls and two strikes. We were in the bottom of the ninth inning and Nolan Ryan, Randy Johnson and Roger Clemens were all warming up.

After everyone left, Max and I just sat there in silence for a few minutes. By now we were like an old married couple. We had gotten so close that silence didn't bother us. It wasn't awkward. We sat there thinking the same thing. We were screwed.

"Max, let's do this. I'm completely burned out. I know you are as well. Tomorrow is Christmas Eve. Let's take the next couple of days off. Let's noodle on what we are going to do. I'll call you on Boxing Day and we'll figure it out. Give me a hug. I need one."

Max stood up and gave me a big, long hug. The kind that says everything is going to be alright. The kind where you can transfer all of your negative energy, emotions, and whatever ails you so that when you let go, you immediately feel better.

"I love you, bro." We both said it to each other and walked out.

CHAPTER 23

David vs. Goliath (Part Two)

I sat on the train ride home completely numb. I had worked my butt off for the last year. Max and I were almost there. We had toiled, sweated, and bled to put this deal together. Had we been able to pull it off, we would have been legends. They would have written books about us and made videos to show the rest of the sales teams. I sat there like a zombie – completely lifeless. No different than the daily commuters around me.

Later that night.

I had gotten into a good routine at karate. I went three times a week and was getting pretty good at it. I had breezed through my first few belts. Everyone at the dojo was impressed that I was making progress so quickly. Of course, it's not that hard to impress 14-year-olds. I actually found it therapeutic to go to karate class. It was high-intensity and anaerobic. By the end of every class I was completely drenched in sweat. All my frustrations, emotions, and negativity were completely and literally beaten out of me.

I had a love/hate relationship with sparring. This is where the rubber meets the road. Sparring is when you put all your basic forms and techniques together. You fight an opponent and the intent is to get as many points as possible. You can only hit in certain areas to get those points. That demonstrates that you have technique and control. This also ensures that you don't actually hurt your opponent. The biggest part about sparring is to overcome your fears of getting hit. Once you overcome that fear, the rest becomes easy.

One of the first concepts they teach you in karate or martial arts is chi. This is your life force or spirit. To enhance, amplify, or show your spirit in karate training, we do what's called a "kiai." A kiai is a short yell or show of spirit. When you launch an attack or strike, if you want to show spirit, you kiai. That means you strike and say "kiai" at the same time. When most kids are performing techniques or sparring, their kiai is weak. Most of the time you can't even hear it. When you see the masters do it, they scare the bejesus out of you. It is loud and guttural. Whenever a master or black belt kiais in class, everyone freezes for a second because it is so visceral. It actually scares you.

I found out early on that if I mimic the masters, it actually works. You scare your opponent. In that split second when they freeze, you can hit them and score a point. Granted, I was sparring with kids, so it was easy to scare them. My sparring opponent tonight was an Indian boy named Jaspal Singh. His friends called him Jesse. Tonight, we would go the distance.

As we were putting on our sparring gear, I looked at him in disbelief. I didn't believe Jesse was a kid and I didn't believe he was only 16 years old. I don't know what they were feeding him at home, but it definitely wasn't a vegan diet. Jesse towered over me at 6'3" and you can tell he went to the GoodLife Fitness gym down the street in his spare time – which was every day, because he didn't have a part-time job.

I love Sensei Mike, but tonight I loved him a little less. For the last few weeks I had been winning my sparring matches by scaring the little kids with my kiais. So, he decided to even the score. Tonight, he was making me spar with Jesse. I was only a blue belt. Jesse was a brown belt and had been at the dojo for four years now.

We touched gloves. Bam, bam, bam. Before I could move, he had hit me three times. I bobbed and weaved. Jab, fake left and upper cut. I might as well have done it in slow motion. He saw it a mile away, yawned, and tapped me on the head like I was a Smurf. Cornered, I resorted to my tried and true secret weapon. I let out a loud kiai. Shit. It didn't scare him one bit. For the next six minutes, I just sucked it up and let him kick the crap out of me. What else would you do if your name was David and you ran into your sworn enemy, Goliath? There is nothing more humbling than being a grown man and getting your butt kicked by a 16-year-old. By the end of the match, I was heaving and drenched in sweat. Emotionally and physically, I was spent. I went home with my head held low. I showered and then collapsed in bed. I hoped tomorrow was going to be a better day.

CHAPTER 24

The Comeback

I was nervous. I was in BUC's washroom near the receptionist area on their executive floor. I was washing my hands and I looked in the mirror. I noticed the bags under my eyes. That was so sad. When was the last time you saw an Asian with bags under his eyes? It never happens. We don't age. The fact that I had them meant that it had been a brutal few months. Alright, I was stalling. Whatever happened, happened. There was nothing I could do about it now. It was time to pay the piper.

"Alright, boys. It's show time." I led my team into BUC's massive Cisco Telepresence room. All of BUC's executives looked refreshed from the Christmas break. We shook hands and greeted everyone. I hid my nervousness and was as smooth as silk. "Randy, let me introduce you to Nathan

Cameroon. Nathan just flew in from California late last night."

"Randy, I'm looking forward to working with your team to resolve these issues. I'm confident we can come to some middle ground," Nathan said as he extended his hand in a gesture of goodwill.

When you see greatness, you recognize it immediately because it is so extreme. When you see Michael Jordan, Wayne Gretzky or Joe Montana play their respective sports, you know you are witnessing something special. They are doing something that no one else can do. And they do it with such finesse and style that they make it look easy. And you know it's not that easy, because otherwise everyone else would be doing as well. Watching Nathan work was like watching Michael, Wayne, or Joe play. He was so good, he made me grin from ear to ear.

While everyone was enjoying the holidays and spending time with their families and counting their blessings, Max and I were working 12-hour days with Nathan, dissecting the different issues and getting to the essence of what BUC was trying to do and how we could potentially agree to it. It had been a feverish week, but we had finally pulled it together. I was feeling better about the situation. When we came back in January, we were going to come back with a vengeance. Max and I focused on all of the points that BUC brought up as outstanding issues. Nathan walked us through different options on how we could address their concerns. Nathan also made sure we had executive air cover. Behind the scenes, he talked to every senior executive at Nano to make sure that everyone was on board to give BUC the terms and conditions that they were looking for.

"I know we have a lot of issues to cover today. Let's start with data protection, as that seems to be the most contentious. Can we go to Section 3, sub-section A, romanette iii?" Nathan started his magic. Silence. "You have particular issues with the second sentence. Can I ask you to articulate with a degree of specificity the issues so that we can address them?"

I started to smile. We had hooked up Nathan's laptop to the projector. Everyone was seeing his desktop. He was asking questions, digesting the feedback, and making changes to the document in real time so that everyone could see it. He was carving up the sentences with the precision of an accomplished surgeon. After two hours, we finally called a bio break.

"Trong, this is fantastic. You guys finally brought the right players who can make the decisions for us to get over this hump. Good job." Sean smacked me on the back as he walked to the men's washroom.

I waved to Max. He knew the signal. We walked to a private area and chatted. He felt the same way that I did. We were both ecstatic. Nathan was exactly what we needed. Our hard work, blood, sweat, and tears were finally starting to pay off. We were starting to see the light at the end of the tunnel.

By 5 pm, everyone was physically and emotionally wiped. We had gone line by line and gotten through 60% of the contentious issues. Nathan was scheduled to be in town for the rest of the week to help us get through the contracts. At the pace we were going, we would be done by the end of the next day. We agreed to convene the next morning at 9 am. I started to feel my shoulders slowly loosen up. The weight had been lifted. It was time to let off some steam.

"Boys, let's got to the bar. Let's celebrate!"

CHAPTER 25

Winning The Bank

Two months later.

I dragged myself out of bed. Willed myself to move the legs and body that didn't want to move. I felt like a dead man walking. My body knew what was going to happen today and it wanted no part of it. Subconsciously, my body knew today was the end. I woke up blah, blue, and sad. I was borderline depressed. It happens every time a relationship comes to an end.

Max and I had chased BUC with a vengeance. All we had done was eat, sleep, and think about BUC. We had done it for the better part of 18 months and had finally realized our dreams. After Nathan left, we had still spent another two months negotiating all the final details to the business and financial terms of our deal. I should have been the happiest guy in the world yet here I was, unable to get out of bed. Every time I had closed a major deal in the past, I had gone through the same emotions. Deep down, I like the thrill of the chase more than the win. It's the high highs and low lows that make it so fun and worthwhile. And when you finally win the deal, the chase and pursuit come to a natural end. Figuratively speaking, it is the end of that relationship.

I had my outfit already picked out: Power blue suit, white Nordstrom's shirt, and a red tie to go with it. I could have been the poster boy for the Republican convention. Psych yourself up. Pull yourself together, man. Put that game face on.

When I walked into the downtown office, I fist-bumped and high-fived everyone. They said congrats. I was shaking hands and kissing babies. I saw Max and we decided to go to Starbucks. It was 11 am and we didn't really need a coffee, but it had been our daily ritual for the last six months. We knew it was probably going to be our last one for a while. As we walked through the underground PATH, we talked about all the funny moments of the deal. We laughed at some of our craziness and patted ourselves on the back for getting out of some pretty hairy situations. When push came to shove, we pulled our teams together and got them to do the impossible. Against the backdrop of regulatory and compliance issues in the US and Canada, as well as big company bureaucracy, we were able to move the machine and get a major bank to move to the cloud. This would be something we would tell our kids about.

When we got back to the office, it was still early. Only 11:30 am. We rounded up a few of our core team and went to grab lunch. Over cocktails and sushi, we rehashed more stories and felt proud and grateful. We felt grateful that we had closed a major deal and that we were going to make boatloads of money. That's why we were in sales and why we were all here. We kept the festivities to only one drink. We were going to celebrate properly later. When BUC told us a week ago that all legal negotiations were done and that they were ready to sign the contract, I had asked them if we could take a picture of the signing. Both of our teams had worked hard on this deal and it meant a lot to us. We had asked them if we could memorialize it with a photo op. Randy and Kevin, because they knew how much this meant to us, readily obliged.

At 1:25 pm, we walked into Randy's office. The signing had been designated for 1:30 pm. I had four of my team with me. Max was right beside me. This was our core team that had done everything to make the deal a reality. Randy brought four of his executive team with him as well. We gave the camera to his chief of staff. His VP signed the stack of documents we laid out before him.

"One, two, three, say cheese!" Snap. Snap. Snap. The camera clicked. Max and I high-fived each other. We had just made history. We had just won the bank.

OUTTAKES

Trong circa 1981. I loved St. John's, Newfoundland. The people were the salt of the earth. These were my formative years where I learned to speak English, learned to love books, and more importantly, learned the value of hard work. In church, I prayed that one day I would be rich enough to afford to eat at McDonald's every weekend!

Our first house in St. John's, Newfoundland, Canada. We went from sleeping on the ground in a refugee camp in Malaysia to a three-bedroom townhouse, all thanks to the Catholic Church. We were unbelievably thankful for our good fortune. Fate had given us a second chance at life and we were not going to squander it.

My dad (Duoc) studied hard to become a refrigeration technician. He showed me that a good work ethic and a desire to succeed can overcome most obstacles.

We packed up in our van and made our way to our new home in Toronto, Canada. We were sad to leave St. John's, Newfoundland and had no idea what was in store for us.

Shawn and his wife Loretta Dobbin, our guardian angels, visiting our new home in Scarborough, Ontario.

Trong (front row, second from left) circa 1989 at Brebeuf College in Toronto. We were "encouraged" to join athletic endeavors as part of our curriculum. I ran cross country and track & field. I consistently came in last place but learned a valuable life lesson – never give up!

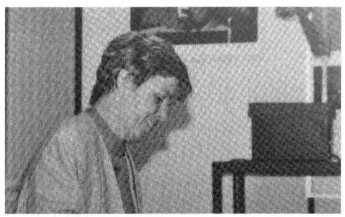

Mrs. Coughlin tutoring Trong in Latin class. I was determined to master the foundations of English.

Trong and Mrs. Coughlin reunited twenty-five years later. She thought she was teaching him Latin. The whole time he was just trying to master English.

Trong Nguyen

AFTERWORD

Somewhere on the journey of life, I realized that you are who you are because of all your experiences along the way – good and bad. I'm thankful that my family had a second chance; I'm thankful for the work ethic that my parents instilled in me; and I'm thankful that I grew up dirt poor. It gave me the drive and motivation to get me where I am today.

It's not hard to know where you are going if you know where you came from. You just have to have the conviction to chase your dreams and make it a reality.

Cheers and Good Selling!

ACKNOWLEDGEMENTS

This book would not have been possible without the expert editing of Cabrina Attal, Kathy Clolinger, Carrie Wujek and Rachel Roberts.

Thank you, Pia Reyes, for the awesome book cover design.

Thanks to the Catholic Church for its commitment to help those that are in need.

Thanks to the amazing Newfies that became our family and friends in St. John's, Newfoundland. You are the kindest people in the world.

Thanks to Canada for opening your arms and borders to immigrants and refugees who need a new place to call home. That's just one of the reasons why Canada is among the best places in the world.

Thanks for reading my second book! Please add a short review on Amazon and let me know what you think!

ABOUT THE AUTHOR

Trong has more than twenty years of experience in sales, marketing, and consulting with the world's largest enterprises across various market segments, including healthcare, telecommunications, insurance, and financial services. Trong honed his craft at DEC, IBM, Dell and Microsoft. Trong earned his Bachelor of Arts degree in Economics from Western University as well as an MBA from The University of Chicago.

You can reach Trong at:
www.linkedin.com/in/megatrong

→ Exec Admins → selling
everywhere ⇕

→ Drinking Trick

→ ability to strategize &
overcome the "Frozen middle"
neutralize

→ selling "Hoped Dreams"
not technology

Sell is solution
Lead up
Services

→ Briefly on
transformation
not technology

→ navigation of
complex politics
→ ultimate strategist.

96428901R00085

Made in the USA
Columbia, SC
27 May 2018